LAST
LAUGHS

FUNNY TOMBSTONE QUOTES
AND FAMOUS LAST WORDS

KATHLEEN E. MILLER

Sterling Publishing, Co., Inc.
New York

To my uncle Raymond Marcinkowski of Waterford, Wisconsin,
who died during the compilation of this volume, and who
used to count the freckles on my nose.
Zawsze.

Library of Congress Cataloging-in-Publication Data

Last laughs : funny tombstone quotes and famous last words /
[compiled by] Kathleen E. Miller.
p. cm.
Includes bibliographical references.
ISBN-13: 978-1-4027-2969-0
ISBN-10: 1-4027-2969-3
1. Last words. 2. Epitaphs. 3. Death--Humor. I. Miller, Kathleen E.

PN6328.L3L26 2006
082--dc22

2006004776

10 9 8 7 6 5 4 3 2

Published by Sterling Publishing Co., Inc.
387 Park Avenue South, New York, NY 10016
© 2006 by Kathleen E. Miller
Distributed in Canada by Sterling Publishing
c/o Canadian Manda Group, 165 Dufferin Street
Toronto, Ontario, Canada M6K 3H6
Distributed in the United Kingdom by GMC Distribution Services
Castle Place, 166 High Street, Lewes, East Sussex, England BN7 1XU
Distributed in Australia by Capricorn Link (Australia) Pty. Ltd.
P.O. Box 704, Windsor, NSW 2756, Australia

Manufactured in the United States

Sterling ISBN-13: 978-1-4027-2969-0
ISBN-10: 1-4027-2969-3

For information about custom editions, special sales, premium and
corporate purchases, please contact Sterling Special Sales
Department at 800-805-5489 or specialsales@sterlingpub.com.

Illustrations taken from *1800 Woodcuts by Thomas Bewick and His School*, edited by
Blanche Cirker, Dover Publications, and *Dore Spot Illustrations: A Treasury from His
Masterworks*, edited by Carol Belanger Grafton, Dover Pictorial Archive Series.

Book design and typesetting by Evan Johnston

Acknowledgments ❧

I'd like to thank Sterling Publishing and Abby Rabinowitz, for choosing me for this project, and Michael Cea for working on it;

Love and thanks to: Joseph D. Lafleur III, for putting up with me while I hacked away at the keyboard most weekends for the past six months; flipping through books for me, doing cemetery drive-bys, and keeping me fed and the kitchen clean;

My parents, Russ & Joan Miller, for adding some of the gems in these pages and for their undying love and support in whatever endeavor I decide to undertake, (although I managed to weasel out of gymnastics, ballet, organ lessons, and I think accordion lessons, before the age of twelve);

Christina Ruby and Shari Maletsky, for freeing me of the drudgery of my home office and bringing me into the 21st-century by lending their laptops; John Maxie, for reminding me that just because you have a laptop doesn't mean you can function properly in the 21st-century; Bonnie Mullin, for a desperately needed, last minute run to the Library of Congress;

Erin McKean, Editor of *Verbatim* magazine for giving me my first publish, and Abbott "Kit" Combes of *The New York Times Magazine*, for giving me my second; William Safire, of *The New York Times*, who taught me how not to write and gave me six years of much appreciated mentoring;

and Joseph D. Lafleur, who let me hold his cabin hostage four weekends in a row—most of these words were written while listening to the Shenandoah river roll by.

CONTENTS

INTRODUCTION ✤

*D*eath isn't funny, which is exactly why we sometimes need to laugh in its face. This is the reason why we happily chime in the Munchkin's refrain, "Ding Dong the Witch is dead!" This is why children dance around singing "Ring Around the Rosy" (which references the bubonic plague) and chant "The worms crawl in, the worms crawl out, the worms play pinochle on your snout!" with no sense of impropriety whatsoever.

Death stalks us from the moment we are born, and we all know that someday, somehow, we will have to confront our own mortality. In this final feud, why shouldn't we have the last word? Hence: the epitaph.

For the epitaph writer, the possibilities are endless. Most people choose to document the deceased's name, date of birth and date of death, and a touching reminder of his or her family role ("beloved mother" or "devoted husband"). Many people write a simple a catch-phrase or a brief comment on how the deceased lived his or her life.

And then there are the bold, brash, or oblivious few who author epitaphs that are purposefully, unwittingly, or just plain funny. Some, like this epitaph from Uniontown, Pennsylvania, make us laugh despite ourselves:

> Here lies the body of
> Jonathan Blake
> Stepped on the gas pedal
> Instead of the brake.

There are epitaphs that manage to cram years of resentment into a few short lines:

> Here lies Ned
> There is nothing more to be said
> Because we like to speak well of the dead
> ANON.

Or just one line:

I don't want to talk about it now.
BONNIE ANDERSON, FOREST LAWN CEMETERY,
HOLLYWOOD HILLS, LOS ANGELES, CA

The epitaphs of those who were famous in life are particularly fascinating for their necessary brevity (you can, after all, only fit so much onto a slab of stone). Bette Davis may take the cake with her epitaph, "She did it the hard way." In Death we are all equal. As glorious as you may be while alive, in death we are all nothing more than, as Benjamin Franklin put it in his proposed epitaph for himself, "food for worms."

The following is a collection of amusing epitaphs, many true, many suspect, that grace the tombs of those who have gone before. They're taken from sources both new and old, from the 21st century to the 17th. Some are funny in their bluntness, others in their grammatical or semantic errors, still others in the realization that our encounters with our neighbors and relations, positive or poisonous, are what we are most remembered for. Some make us laugh with their brief and brilliant statements on the fleeting circumstance of life.

But each one, even the ones that exist only anecdotally, makes an indelible contribution to our folklore and reminds us that not only must we *Memento Mori* ("remember you must die") but that "life is a jest"—a truth we will all discover in due time.

NOTE: Many of the sources are repetitive, and, as with any story, some of them change as they are passed along through the ages. That's why some of the epitaphs you'll find here have different versions, supposedly in several different states, or even countries, or varying spellings and names. Unfortunately, due to time and weather (even vandalism), many of the older epitaphs are no longer verifiable.

ONE

EVERY
WHICH
WAY

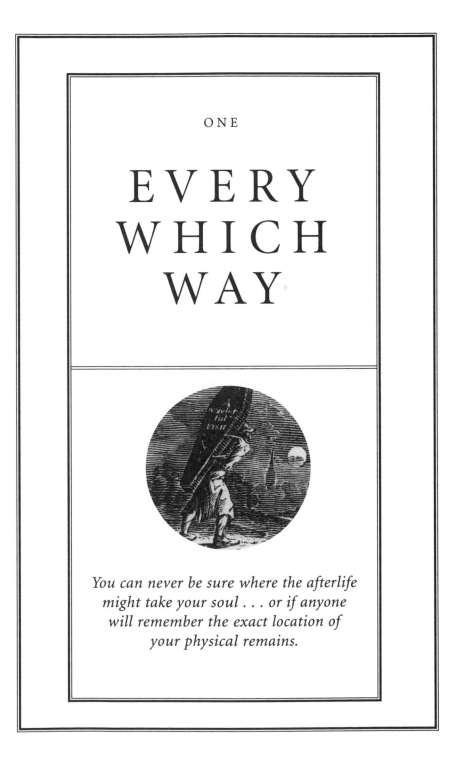

*You can never be sure where the afterlife
might take your soul . . . or if anyone
will remember the exact location of
your physical remains.*

William Sherwood
Died 1682
Here lyeth William Sherwood
That was born in the parish
Of White Chappell near London
A Great Sinner waiting for
a Joyfull Resurrection
William Sherwood, Jamestown, Virginia.

He might have to wait a while.

☾

When the great judgment day arrives
And Joshua Newton Fenton does
Not emerge from this hole.
You will know that someone made a
Mistake and buried me
In the wrong hole.
Joshua Fenton
Location unknown, obviously

❦

I am safe in saying
She's gone up higher
Nary a devil would want Maria
Anonymous, Ubley Church,
Somerset, England

❧

Here lies old twenty percent,
The more he got the less he spent,
The more he got the more he craved,
If he's gone to Heaven, we'll all be saved.
Anonymous, New York, New York

Strange is my name,
And I'm on strange ground
And strange it is
I can't be found.

WILLIAM STRANGE, SOMEWHERE IN WEST VIRGINIA

To the memory of
Thomas Hanse
Lord, thy grace is free
Why not for me?
And the Lord answered & said:
Because thy debts ain't paid.

THOMAS HANSE, COGGESHALL, ESSEX, ENGLAND

Here lies Bessy Bell
But whereabouts I cannot tell.

ANONYMOUS, SOMEWHERE IN A NECROPOLIS IN SCOTLAND

In this churchyard lies Eppie Coutts,
Either here or hereabouts;
But where it is none can tell
Till Eppie herself rise and tell.

EPPIE COUTTS, TORRYBURN CHURCHYARD, ENGLAND

GODFREY HILL, AET 46.
—Thus far am I got on my journey;
READER:
Canst thou inform me
What follows next?

GODFREY HILL, ST. PANCRAS CHURCHYARD, ENGLAND

Ten in the hundred lies here engraved;
'Tis a hundred to ten his soul is not saved;
If any man asks who lies in this tomb
"Oh-o!" quoth the devil, "tis my John-a-comb."
Mr. Combe, who supposedly
has written Shakespeare's plays

~

*This one supposedly graces many a tomb, usually an
afterthought written by a family member:*

Gone home below
And the afterthought:

To follow you I'm not content,
Unless I know which way you went.
Anonymous, Grafton, Vermont

☾

He thought of course his holdings must
Admit him to the heavenly Trust—
But when he handed in his proxy,
He found they wanted orthodoxy.
Anonymous

❧

Here lies a poor woman who was always tired
She lived in a house where help wasn't hired
The Last words she said were "Dear Friends,
I am going where washing ain't wanted,
Nor mending nor sewing
There all things is done exact to my wishes
Where folks don't eat there's no need for dishes,
In Heaven loud anthems forever are ringing
But having no voice, I'll keep clear of singing
Don't mourn for me now, don't mourn for me never
I'm going to do nothing forever and ever."
Anonymous, Pembroke, Massachusetts

I have transplanted a large portion to heaven in acts of charity,
And have gone thither to enjoy it.
Estella Shipley, location unknown

❧

I came I now not whence,
I go I know not whither
Charles A. Miller,
Siloam Cemetery,
Vineland, New Jersey, 1905

∼

Born in Fitzwilliam, N.H., April 3, 1829
Died in Putnam, Ct. May 2, 1918
Going, But Know Not Where.
Phineas Gardner Wright,
Putnam, Connecticut

☾

Here lies the bones
Of Joseph Jones
Who ate whilst he was able:
But once o'erfed
He dropped down dead
And fell beneath the table.
Then from his tomb,
To meet his doom
He rises amidst sinners;
Since he must dwell
In Heaven or Hell
Take him, which gives the best dinners.
Joseph Jones,
Wolverhampton Churchyard,
Staffordshire, England, 1690

Beneath this plain pine board is laying the
Body of Joshua Hight
'Cheer up,' the parson told him dying
'Your future's very bright.'
Slowly the sick man raised his head
His weeping friends amazing
'Parson, it's most too bright,' he said
'For I can see it blazing'
JOSHUA HIGHT,
LOCATION UNKNOWN

❧

Ebenezer Dockwood
Aged forty-seven
A miser and a hypocrite
And never went to heaven
EBENEZER DOCKWOOD,
LOCATION UNKNOWN

❧

. . . .In the resurrection morn, if I have to go below
I'll grab my jug, and fill it with water on the road down
They say they need water down below.
S.P. DINSMOOR, LUCAS, KANSAS, INSTRUCTIONS ON
PUTTING AN EMPTY JUG IN HIS CASKET, 1932

☾

Daniel E. Cole
Born Feb 2, 1844
Went Away
March 22, 1921
I wonder where he went
DANIEL E. COLE, WELLSBORO,
PENNSYLVANIA

In this here grave ye see before ye,
Lies buried up a dismal story;
A young maiden she wor crossed in love,
And tooken to the realms above
But he that crossed her I should say,
Deserves to go t'other way.
ANONYMOUS, PETEWAN,
CORNWALL, ENGLAND

✖

Gone to meet his mother-in-law
ANONYMOUS
I wonder where exactly his mother-in-law went. All rests upon
whether he, or his wife, wrote the epitaph, doesn't it?

↬

Too bad for heaven, too good for Hell
So, where he's gone, I cannot tell
ANONYMOUS

〰

She died, poor dear, of disappointed love
And angels bore her soul to the realms above
When her young man is summoned, so they say
He will be carried off the other way.
ANONYMOUS

☾

Here lyes the body and the banes
Of the Laird of Whinkerstanes;
He was neither gud to rich nor puir,
But now the de'il has him sure
FOGO CHURCHYARD,
BERWICKSHIRE, ENGLAND

Here lies the carcass
Of a cursed sinner
Doomed to be roasted
For the Devil's dinner
ANONYMOUS

❧

Stranger
Beneath this cone in
UNCONSECRATED
Ground
A friend to the liberties
Of Mankind
Directed his body to be inurned
May the example contribute
To the emancipation of thy mind
From the idle fears of
SUPERSTITION
And the wicked arts
Of Priesthood
JOHN BASKERVILLE, BIRMINGHAM, ENGLAND

Well, then—tell us how you really feel.

TWO

PITHY
AND
PUNNY

*It's never too late to have
a sense of humor, intentional or not.*

Dr. Thomas Bart
1803–1860
The operation was successful
THOMAS BART, PAWTUCKET, RHODE ISLAND
If ending up dead was the intended outcome of "the operation,"
we're probably better off that Dr. Bart is no longer with us.

☾

Goodbye, Jim
Take ker of yourself.
ANONYMOUS, EDMONTON, ALBERTA, CANADA

❦

If your nose is close to the grindstone
And you hold it there long enough
In time you'll say there's no such thing
As brooks that babble and birds that sing
These three will all your world compose—
Just you, the stone and your poor old nose.
ANONYMOUS, FALSGRAVE PARISH CHURCH, SCARBOROUGH,
YORKSHIRE, ENGLAND

❧

Here lies a man that was Knott born
His father was Knott before him
He lived Knott and died Knott
Yet underneath this stone doth lie.
John Knott, Sheffield, England

∼

Here I lays
Paddy O'Blase
With the tip of my nose
And the points of my toes
Turned up to the roots of the daisies.
PADDY O'BLASE, MONKSTOWN CEMETERY,
COUNTY CORK, IRELAND

Another Irishman is said to have a similar inscription on his tomb in Ballyporen, Ireland:

Teague O'Brien
Here I at length repose
My spirit now at aise is;
With the tips of my toes
And the point of my nose
Turned up to the roots of the daisies.

((

Here lies John Steere,
Who, when living, brewed good beer,
Turn to the right, go down the hill
His son keeps up the business still.
JOHN STEERE, ST. MARY'S CHURCH,
DAGENHAM, ESSEX, ENGLAND

✖

What's that old joke? "And I says to myself, Self!"

As I walked by myself I talked to myself
And thus myself said to me,
Look to thyself and take care of thyself
For nobody cares for thee.
So I turned to myself and I answered myself
In the self-same reverie
Look to myself or look not to myself
The self-same thing will it be.
ROBERT CRYTOFT,
HOMERSFIELD, ENGLAND, 1810

∽

Stephen and Time are now both even,
Stephen beats time and now Time's beaten Stephen
ANONYMOUS MUSIC TEACHER,
ST. IVES, CORNWALL, ENGLAND

Excuse my dust (proposed for herself)
DOROTHY PARKER, 1967

~

And away we go!
*Since this is Jackie Gleason, aka Herbert John Gleason,
it should be read, "and awaaay we go," with the correct intonation.*

☾

I told you I was ill.
SPIKE MILLIGAN, BRILLIANT COMEDIAN OF THE BRITISH STAGE.
THE SENTIMENT IS WRITTEN IN GAELIC.
*Mulligan at one time proposed that the text of his tombstone read: "I
demand a second opinion."*

✄

Here he lies, somewhere.
*Supposedly, suggested for himself, the grave of Werner Karl
Heisenberg, of the Heisenberg Theory who surmised that the location of an electron cannot be assigned a position in space at any
given moment.*

↩

Exit Burbage.
RICHARD BURBAGE, ACTOR,
SOMEWHERE IN ENGLAND

~

Within this tomb lies the world's loveliest rose
But she who was sweet will now offend your nose.
ANONYMOUS, GODSTOW CHURCH,
OXFORD, ENGLAND

☾

She was the sunshine of our home
LYDIA J. MOON, PROVIDENCE CEMETERY,
GRAHAM, NORTH CAROLINA

This guy's hooked on phonics:

In memori ov
Meri Pitman
Weif ov Mr. Eizak Pitman
Fonetik Printer, ov this Siti.
Died 19 August 1857, edjed 64.
"Preper tu mit thei God."
MARY PITMAN, LANSDOWNE CEMETERY,
BATH, SOMERSET, ENGLAND

Whoever treadeth on this stone
I prey you tread most neatly
For underneath this same do lie
Your honest friend—WILL WHEATLEY
WILL WHEATLEY, STEPNEY CEMETERY,
LONDON, ENGLAND

Here's a great waste of good marble:

B.H. Morris
Died April, 1900
Kind friends
I leave behind
Cast your votes
FOR WM. J. BRYAN
BETHEL CEMETERY, SAVANNAH, GEORGIA

I bowl'd, I struck, I caught, I stopp'd
Sure life's a game of cricket;
I block'd with care, with caution popp'd
Yet Death has hit my wicket.
ANONYMOUS CRICKET PLAYER,
SALISBURY, WILTSHIRE, ENGLAND

"Out"
at 90.
ANOTHER CRICKET PLAYER, LOCATION AND NAME UNKNOWN

☾

Though hot my name, yet mild my nature
I bore good will to every creature;
I brewed good ale and sold it too,
And unto each I gave his due.
WILLIAM PEPPER,
ST. JOHN'S, STAMFORD, ENGLAND, 1783

❦

Death took him in the *upper* View
And gave him such a *Brace*,
The grapple turn'd him black and blue,
And made him shift his place.
Parts of Access he next assailed,
With suck a *Knock-down blow*
As never yet a mortal fail'd
A total overthrow.
A WRESTLER,
LONDON, ENGLAND

❦

Here lies an Old Toss' Tennis Ball,
Was racketed from Spring to Fall
With so much heat and so much blast
Time's arm (for shame) grew tyr'd at last
GERVASE SCROPE, COVENTRY CEMETERY,
WARWICKSHIRE, ENGLAND

❦

Cheerful in death I close my eyes
Into thy arms, My God, I flies.
ANONYMOUS, UNVERIFIED

Underneath this crust,
Lies the mouldering dust of
Eleanor Batchelor Shoven,
Well versed in the arts
Of pies, custards and tarts,
And the lucrative trade of the oven.
When she lived long enough
She made her last puff,
A puff by her husband much praised,
And now she doth lie
And make a dirt pie,
In hopes that her crust may be raised.
ELEANOR SHOVEN,
WHITBY PARISH CHURCH,
YORKSHIRE, ENGLAND

☾

Stranger! Behold interred together
The souls of learning and of leather
Poor Joe is gone, but left his awl
You'll find his relics in a stall.
JOSEPH BLACKETT,
SEAHAM PARISH CHURCH,
DURHAM, ENGLAND

❧

Here lies a man, as God shall me save,
Whose mouth was wide, as is his grave;
Reader, tread lightly o'er his sod,
For if he gapes, you're gone, by God.
ANONYMOUS, REPORTED IN COLESHILL,
WARWICKSHIRE, ENGLAND

Another man, with a similarly big mouth:

Old Thomas Mulvaney lies here
His mouth ran from ear to ear
Reader, tread lightly on this wonder
For if he yawns, you're gone by thunder
MIDDLEFORD, MASSACHUSETTS, 1795

❧

Here lies a marksman, who with art and skill,
When young and strong, fat bucks and does did kill.
Now conquered by grim Death (go, reader, tell!)
He's now took leave of powder, gun and pellet.
A fatal dart, which in the dark did fly,
Has laid him down, among the dead to lie.
ANONYMOUS, REVENGLASS PARISH CHURCH,
WESTMORELAND, ENGLAND

〰

This tombstone is a milestone;
Hah! How so?
Because beneath lies MILES
Who's miles below.
A little man he was, a dwarf in size,
Yet now stretched out, at least Miles long he lies
This grave, though small, contains a space so wide
There's Miles in breadth and length and room beside.
MR. MILES, WEBLEY CHURCHYARD,
YORKSHIRE, ENGLAND

Here lies the Earl of Suffolk's fool;
Men called him DICKY PEARCE;
His folly serv'd to make men laugh,
When wit and mirth were scarce.
Poor Dick, alas! Is dead and gone,
What signifies to cry?
Dicky's enough are still behind
To laugh at by and by.
BECKLEY CHURCH, SUFFOLK, ENGLAND

☾

Wha lies here?
I Johnnie Dow.
Hoo Johnnie is that you?
Ay, man, but I'm dead now.
JOHNNIE DOW, ST. DECUMAN'S,
SOMERSETSHIRE, ENGLAND

🐌

This is to the memory of OLD AMOS
Who was when alive for hunting famous;
But now his chases are all o'er
And here he's earth'd of years four score.
Upon this tomb he often sat
And tried to read his epitaph;
And thou who dost so at this moment
Shall ere long like him be dormant.
AMOS STREET, BIRSTAL CHURCHYARD, ENGLAND

🙚

Curious enough, we all must say,
That what was stone should now be clay;
Must curious still, to own we must,
That what was stone must soon be dust.
MISS STONE, MELTON MOWBRAY CHURCHYARD,
LEICESTERSHIRE, ENGLAND

Here lies Tommy Montague
Whose love for angling daily grew;
He died regretted, while late out,
To make a capture of a trout.
ANONYMOUS, SUTTON MALLET CEMETERY,
SOMERSET, ENGLAND

Alack and well a-day
Potter himself is turned to clay
DR. POTTER, THE ARCHBISHOP
OF CANTERBURY, 1736

Since I have been so quickly done for
I wonder what I was begun for.
ANONYMOUS

So died JOHN SO
So so did he so?
So did he live
And So did he die;
So so did he so?
And so let him lie.
ST. JOHN'S CHURCH,
GLASGOW, SCOTLAND

Here lies
JOHN TAGGART
of honest fame,
of stature low
&
a leg lame
Content he was
with portion small
kept a shop in Wigtown
&
that's all
JOHN TAGGART, WIGTOWN,
GALLOWAY, SCOTLAND

Reader, don't smile!
But reflect at this tombstone you view,
That death, who kill'd him, in a very short while
Will huddle a stone upon you.
JOHN HUDDLESTONE, LOCATION UNKNOWN

We all must die, there is no doubt
Your glass is running—mine is out.
ANONYMOUS, SHOREDITCH CHURCHYARD

Here lies my corpse, who was the man
That loved a sop in the dripping pan;
But now believe me, I am dead,
See how the pan stands at my head,
Still for the sops till the last I cried
But could not eat, and so I died.
My neighbours, they perhaps will laugh
When they do read my epitaph.
ANONYMOUS, WOODDITTON, SUFFOLK, ENGLAND

For eighteen years
Attached to the United States Navy
Died Dec. 9, 1857 in the 73rd year
Of his age
He spent his life upon the sea
Fighting for the Nation
He doubled his enjoyment
By doubling all his rations.
JAMES ANTHONY, COMMON BURYING GROUND,
NEWPORT, RHODE ISLAND, 1857

✖

In memory of
Benjamin Linton
Blacksmith
Who died Oct. 10. 1842 aged 80
His sledge and hammer
Lie reclin'd his bellows too
Have lost their wind
His fires extinct
His forge decayed
His vice all in the dust is
Laid, his coal is spent
His iron gone
His last nail's driven
His work is done
BENJAMIN LINTON, BLEAN, KENT, ENGLAND

A variation, said to be over the grave of one Samuel Turner from Chipping Sodbury, Gloucestershire reads:

His sledge and hammer lie reclined,
His bellows, too, has lost its wind,
His coal is spent, his iron gone
His nails are drove, his work is done
His body's here, clutched in the dust.
'Tis hoped his soul is with the just

Underneath this stone lies MEREDITH MORGAN
Who blew the bellows of our church organ.
Tobacco he hated, to smoke most unwilling,
Yet never so pleased as when the pipes he was filling.
No reflection on him for rude speech could be cast,
Though he gave our old organ many a blast!
No puffer was he, thought a capital blower;
He could blow double G, and now lies a note lower.
LLANFYLANTWTHYL PARISH CHURCH, WALES

◆

Life's like an Inn
Where traveler's stay
Some only breakfast and away
Others to dinner stay
And are full fed
The oldest only sup
And go to bed
Long is his bill who
Lingers out the day
Who goes the soonest
Has the least to pay
ANONYMOUS

◡

Devoted Christian mother who whipped
Sherman's bummers with scalding water
While trying to take the dinner pot
Which contained a ham bone being
Cooked for her soldier boys
A CONFEDERATE WOMAN,
REBECCA JONES, PLEASANT GROVE CEMETERY,
RALEIGH, NORTH CAROLINA, 1890

Another feisty woman is buried in Ancrum Moor, Roxburgh,
Scotland, where a battle was fought against the British:

Fair Maiden Lillyard lies under this stone
Little was her stature, but great was her fame;
Upon the English lions she laid many thumps
And when her legs were cutted off
She fought on her stumps. *1545*

☽

I dreamt that buried in my fellow clay
Close by a common beggars side I lay;
Such a mean companion hurt my pride
And like a corpse of consequence I cried
Scoundrel be gone, and henceforth touch me not
More manners learn, and at a distance rot.
Scoundrel, in still haughtier tones he cried
Proud lump of earth, I scorn thy words & thee:
All here are equal, thy place is now mine;
This is my rotting place, and that is thine.
JOHN KERR, PROVIDENCE, RHODE ISLAND, 1835

❧

Here lies Roger Rutter, alias Rudder
Eldest son of John Rutter, of Uley,
Who was buried August 30, 1771, aged 84 years
Having never eaten FLESH, FISH, or FOWL
During the course of his long life.
ULEY CHURCHYARD,
GLOUCESTERSHIRE, ENGLAND

❦

Here lies an atheist
All dressed up
And no place to go
THURMONT, MARYLAND,
UNVERIFIED

Here lies Matthew Mudd
Death did him no hurt
When he was alive he was Mudd
But now he's only dirt.
MATTHEW MUDD, WALTON,
NORFOLK, ENGLAND

~

Here lies a Foote
Whose death may thousands save
For Death now has one Foote
Within the grave
ANONYMOUS

☾

In remembrance of that
Prodigy of nature
Daniel Lambert
A native of Leicester
Who was possessed of an
Excellent & convivial mind
& in personal greatness
had no competitor
he measured 3ft 1 inch
round the leg, nine ft 4 in
round the body & weighed 52 stones 11 lbs
He departed this life on the
21st June 1809 aged 39 years
As a testimony of respect
This stone was erected
By his friends in Leicester
DANIEL LAMBERT, ST. MARTIN'S,
STAMFORD, LEICESTER, ENGLAND

By the way, a stone is a measurement equal to 12 pounds!

Here lies John Bunn
He was killed by a gun
His name was not Bunn, but his real name was Wood
But Wood would not rhyme with gun
So I thought Bun Wood.
JOHN WOOD, APPLEBY,
WESTMORELAND, ENGLAND

Another similar verse:

Underneath this pile of stones,
Lies all that's left of Sally Jones.
Her name was Lord, it was not Jones,
But Jones was used to rhyme with stones.
SALLY LORD, SKANEATELES, NEW YORK

❧

This is what I expected but not so soon
WILLIAM REESE, WESTERVILLE, NEW YORK

❧

Papa—did you wind your watch?
CHARLES B. GUNN, A TRAIN ENGINEER,
EVERGRAIN CEMETERY, COLORADO

❧

Here lies
In a horizontal position
The outside case of
THOMAS HINDE
Clock and watchmaker
Who departed this life wound up
In hope of being taken in hand
By his maker and being thoroughly cleaned
And repaired and
Set a-going in the world to come
On the 15th of August 1836
In the 19th year of his age.
THOMAS HINDE, BOLSOVER, DERBYSHIRE, ENGLAND

Seems as if this watchmaker epitaph was a prepared verse:

Here lies, in horizontal position
The outside case of
George Routleigh, watchmaker;
Whose abilities in that line were an honour
To his profession.
Integrity was the mainspring, and prudence
The Regulator,
Of all the actions of his life.
Humane, generous, and liberal,
His Hand never stopped
Till he had relieved distress.
So nicely regulated were all his motions
That he never went wrong,
Except when set a-going
By people
Who did not know his Key:
Even then he was easily
Set right again.
He had the art of disposing his time so well
That his hours glided away
In one continual round
Of pleasure and delight,
Till an unlucky minute put a period to
His existence.
He departed this life
Nov. 24, 1802
Aged 57
Wound up
In hopes of being taken in hand
By his Maker;
And of being thoroughly cleaned, repaired and
Set a-going
In the world to come
GEORGE ROUTLEIGH, LYDFORD CHURCH,
DARTMOOR, DEVON, ENGLAND

The gravestone is carved with the outline of a check:
A new joint account
The bank of Santa Cruz
South Lawn Branch
Pay to the order of POSTERITY
TO BALANCE OF ACCOUNT

☾

Jess G. or Vivian E.
Kinser

Jess_____Vivian
1900–   1906–1967
COPYRIGHTED 1966
JESS G. AND VIVIAN E. KINSER,
SOUTHLAWN CEMETERY, SANTA CRUZ, CALIFORNIA

❦

Reader cash thou art
In want of any
Dig 4 feet deep
And thou wilt find a Penny.
JOHN PENNY, WINBORNE, ENGLAND

☙

Here lyeth JOHN CRUKER, a maker of bellowes
His craft's master and King of good fellows;
Yet when he came to the hour of his death,
He that made bellowes, could not make breath.
JOHN CRUKER, OXFORD, ENGLAND

～

FINAL DECREE
JUSTICE SILAS W. SANDERSON,
SUPREME COURT OF CALIFORNIA, LAUREL HILL CEMETERY,
SAN FRANCISCO, CALIFORNIA

It's the name on this one that gets me:

ASAD EXPERIENCE WILSON
1895–1946
IDLEWILD CEMETERY, HOOD RIVER, OREGON

☾

*Here is an entry that's too good to be true. His name was either
Solomon, Ezekiel or Jonathan and he is buried in St. Alban's;
Pembroke, England; Nantucket, Massachusetts; or Barre, Vermont.
Provenance aside, it's just too clever not to include it:*

He is not here
But only his pod;
He shelled out his peas
And went to God.

Variation number 2:

Under this sod and under these trees
Lies the body of Solomon Pease
He is not here, there's only his pod
Pease shelled out and went to God.

Variation number 3:

Here lies the body of Solomon Pease
Under the daises and the trees;
Pease not here, only the pod,
Pease shelled out and gone to God.

❧

Owen Moore
Gone Away
Owin' More
Than he could pay
OWEN MOORE, ST. JOHN'S CHURCH,
BATTERSEA, LONDON

Here lies one blown out of breath
Who lived a merry life
And died a Merideth.
MR. MERIDETH, WINTON COLLEGE,
OXFORD (AN ORGANIST). HIS NAME IS
ALTERNATELY SPELLED MERIDITH.

~

Gone Fishing
Jan. 19, 1945–Nov. 1, 1994
KENNETH MICHAEL MCMAHON,
LOS ANGELES, CALIFORNIA

~

Once I wasn't
Then I was
Now I ain't again.
ARTHUR C. HOMANS, CLEVELAND, OHIO

☾

Haine Haint
ARTHUR HAINE, CITY CEMETERY,
VANCOUVER, WASHINGTON

~

Jonathan Grober
Died dead sober
Lord, thy wonders never cease
JONATHAN GROBER, CLINKERTON CEMETERY,
NOTTINGHAMSHIRE, ENGLAND

~

The pretty flowers that blossom here
Are fertilized by Gertie Greer
GERTIE GREER, LOCATION UNKNOWN

The defense rests
COUNSELOR JOHN E. GOEMBEL,
WILLWOOD CEMETERY, ROCKFORD, ILLINOIS

Office upstairs
DR. FRED ROBERTS, PHYSICIAN,
PINE LOG CEMETERY, BROOKLAND, ARKANSAS

At last, a year-long resident
ROBERT G. ROGERS, WEST CHOP CEMETERY,
VINEYARD HAVEN, MASSACHUSETTS

The area is famous for people "summering" there.

Born	Died
Tampico, Mexico	Against his better judgment
Oct 14, 1907	March 15, 1983

CHARLES HENRY ROLKER,
LOS ANGELES, CALIFORNIA

I came into this world
Without my consent
And left in the same manner
ANONYMOUS, CHATTANOOGA, TENNESSEE

JOHN ROSEWELL
This graves a bed of roses: here doth lye
John Rosewell, gent., his wife nine children by
JOHN ROSEWELL AND FAMILY,
INGLISHCOMBE, ENGLAND, 1687, AGED 79

Here lies Stephen Rumbold
He lived to the age of one hundred and one
Sanguine and Strong
A hundred to one you don't live so long
STEPHEN RUMBOLD, BRIGHTWELL,
BALDWIN, OXFORDSHIRE, ENGLAND

☾

TRANSPLANTED
LORENZO SABINE, HILLSIDE CEMETERY
EASTPORT, MAINE

🐛

Hurry! The party's started.
1914–1997
ELSA G. SCHAPER, LOS ANGELES, CALIFORNIA

🙰

I made an ash of myself
JULIAN SKAGGS, SOMEWHERE IN WEST VIRGINIA

〜

God knows I tried
ERIC SLOAN, KENT, CONNECTICUT

☾

Here lies an honest lawyer
That is Strange
COUNSELOR JOHN STRANGE,
LOCATION UNKNOWN

Another lawyer:

God works a wonder now and then,
Here, though a lawyer, was an honest man
ANONYMOUS, RINETON CHURCHYARD,
NORFOLK, ENGLAND

Been Here:
Now gone:
Had a good time
1916
DR. J.J. SUBERS, ROSE HILL CEMETERY,
MACON, GEORGIA

❧

Thorpe's Corpse
MR. THORPE, LOCATION UNKNOWN.

It is reported that when Mr. Thorpe's wife died, according to her wishes the tomb was changed to read: Thorpes' Corpses

❧

Here lies Groucho Marx
And Lies and Lies and Lies
p.s. he never kissed an ugly girl
(PROPOSED FOR HIMSELF)

❧

Here lieth W. W.
Who never more will
Trouble you, trouble you
WILLIAM WILSON,
LAMBETH CHURCHYARD, LONDON, ENGLAND

☾

Here lies
Johnny Yeast
Pardon me
For not rising
JOHNNY YEAST, RUIDOSO,
NEW MEXICO

Just minutes away.
ED ZABERER, MAYS LANDING, NEW JERSEY

✣

Oh cruel Death.
To satisfy thy palate
Cut down our lettuce
to make a salad.
LETTUCE MANNING,
LOCATION UNKNOWN

❧

School is out
Teacher has gone home.
PROFESSOR S.B. MCCRACKEN,
ELKHART, INDIANA

∼

Here lie the remains of John Hall, grocer
The world in not worth a fig, and I have
Raisins for saying so.
JOHN HALL, DUNMORE, IRELAND, 1790

☾

Stranger tread
This ground with gravity
Dentist Brown is
Filling his last cavity.
DR. BROWN, ST. GEORGE'S CHURCH,
EDINBURGH, SCOTLAND

✣

Here lies the landlord Tommy Dent
In his last cozy tenement.
TOMMY DENT, ST. STEPHEN CHURCHYARD,
WEST DUFORD, ENGLAND

My trip is ended
Send my samples home
SALESMAN THOMAS W. CAMPBELL,
ASPEN GROVE CEMETERY,
BURLINGTON, IOWA, 1862

❧

*Another where provenance is uncertain, having been placed in
either Hartscombe, England or somewhere in New Jersey:*

On the 22 of June
Jonathan Fiddle
Went out of tune.

Here's a variation:

Here lies the body of Jonathan Fiddle
In 1868, on the 30th day of June
He went out of tune.

～

Peas to his hashes;
LONGRIDGE CEMETERY, PRESTON,
LANCASHIRE, ENGLAND
Meaning of course, Peace to his ashes.

☾

Here lies the body, late Mayor of Dundee
Here lies him, here lies he
A.B.C.D.E.F.G.
Di Do Dum, Di Do Dee
ANONYMOUS, DUNDEE, SCOTLAND

❦

These two tombstones are found side by side:

Here I lie snug as a bug in a rug   Here I lie snugger than that other bugger
ANONYMOUS,
LOCATION UNKNOWN

Thomas Gardiner
Historian of Southwald and Denwich
Buried with his two wives, Honor and Virtue
Between Honor and Virtue, here doth lie
The remains of old Antiquity.
THOMAS GARDINER,
SOUTHWOLD, ENGLAND, 1750

❦

He's done a-catching cod
And gone to meet his God
CAPT. THOMAS COFFIN,
NEW SHOREHAM,
RHODE ISLAND, 1842

∼

Poor John Scott
Lies buried here
Though once he was
Both hale and stout
Now Death has drawn
His bitter bier
Now in a better world
He hops about
BREWER JOHN SCOTT,
ST. GEORGE'S PARISH CHURCH,
LIVERPOOL, ENGLAND

To the memory of John Higgs
Pig Killer
Who died November 26th, 1825
Aged 55 years
Here lies John Higgs
A famous man for killing pigs
For killing pigs was his delight
Both morning, afternoon, & night
Both heats & cold he did endure
Which no physician could cure
His knife is laid his work is done
I hope to heaven his soul has gone
JOHN HIGGS, CHELTENHAM PARISH CHURCH,
GLOUCESTERSHIRE, ENGLAND

Here is another rendition:

Here lies a true and honest man,
You scarce would find such a one in ten;
For killing pigs was his delight,
Which art he practiced day and night.

☾

Worms are bait for fish
But here's a sudden change
Fish is bait for worms
Is that not passing strange?
A MAN NAMED FISH, LOCATION UNKNOWN

🐿

Here lies
JAMES EARL
The pugilist
Who on the
11th April 1788
gave in
JAMES EARL, BATTERSEA CEMETERY,
LONDON, ENGLAND

Sh-h-h
THOMAS O. MURPHY,
MOUNTAIN VIEW CEMETERY,
VANCOUVER, CANADA

❧

MEL BLANC
Man of 1,000 voices
Beloved Husband and Father
1908–1989
"That's All Folks"
MEL BLANC, HOLLYWOOD MEMORIAL PARK,
LOS ANGELES, CALIFORNIA

Mel was the famous voice behind many of the Warner Brothers characters, such as Daffy Duck and Bugs Bunny.

～

Beloved wife, mother, and grandmother
"What goes around comes around"
Aug 13, 1915   Aug. 7, 1994
JEAN "COOKIE" BERMER
LOS ANGELES, CALIFORNIA

☾

"This is on me, boys."
WILLIAM P. ROTHWELL,
OAK GROVE CEMETERY, PAWTUCKET,
RHODE ISLAND, 1939

❧

She did it the hard way.
BETTE DAVIS, FOREST LAWN CEMETERY,
HOLLYWOOD, CALIFORNIA

I wonder if "doing it the hard way" means having cat fights with Joan Crawford.

World Famous
Answered his last curtain call
Sept. 19, 1946
ALEXANDER CARR,
LOS ANGELES, CALIFORNIA

Another actor:

Oh, sad to tell
On Mrs. Monks
The curtain last has fell.
ANONYMOUS, STRATFORD CEMETERY,
LONDON, ENGLAND

❧

He has answered
His last alarm
A FIREFIGHTER,
WILLIAM P. MONROE,
WILMINGTON, NORTH CAROLINA

〜

1938–1996
God Bless his soul
He was a tootsie roll
But now he's a dead cat, just the same
JOHNNY D. FLYNN,
LOCATION UNKNOWN

☾

Fuzzy Woodruff
1884–1929
"Copy all in"
FAMOUS SPORTSWRITER LORENZO FERGUSON,
BURIED UNDER HIS PSEUDONYM IN CROWN HILL CEMETERY,
ATLANTA, GEORGIA

May ye be an hour in Heaven before the devil knows you're dead.
DONNA JEAN FARRELL, FOREST LAWN,
CYPRESS, CALIFORNIA

❧

The dust of
Melantha Gribbling
Swept up at last
By the
Great Housekeeper.
LOCATION UNKNOWN

❧

Two things I love most
Good horses and beautiful women
And when I die I hope they tan
This old hide of mine and make it
Into a ladies riding saddle, so
I can rest between the two things
I love most.
RUSSELL J. LARSON,
LOGAN CITY CEMETERY, LOGAN, UTAH

~

Here lies the body of Dr. Bowen,
Caught when death was out a mowin'
Used to curing others ills—
Yet his homeopathic pills
Couldn't keep the Doc from going'
DR. BOWEN, LOCATION UNKNOWN

☾

Sacred to the memory of George Mutton
Who surfeited himself with eating bacon
It's a very surprising thing to me
That mutton and bacon can't agree.
GEORGE MUTTON, NORTH BUCKLAND, ENGLAND, 1750

Here I lie at the chancel door
Here I lie because I'm poor
The farther in the more you pay
Here I lie as warm as they.
ROBERT PHILLIP, KINGSBRIDGE,
DEVON, ENGLAND

The owner of this grave was supposedly the gravedigger for the parish.

❧

Here lies Robert Trollope
Who made your stones roll up.
When Death took his soul up
His body fill'd this hole up.
ROBERT TROLLOPE,
GATESHEAD, ENGLAND

❧

This we must own in justice to her shade
This the first bad exit Oldfield ever made.
ACTRESS MRS. OLDFIELD,
BRIXTON, LONDON, ENGLAND

The tombstone is spurious.

❧

Getting there is half the fun.
SAMUEL J. McKELVEY,
MOUNT PLEASANT CEMETERY,
TORONTO, CANADA

☾

None of us ever voted for Roosevelt or Truman.
HALLENBECK,
ROBERT AND FAMILY,
ELGIN, MINNESOTA

Whoe'er you are, tread softly,
I entreat you
For if he chance to wake,
be sure he'll eat you.
PETER RANDOLPH,
LOCATION UNKNOWN

❧

Bury me not when I am dead
Lay me not down in a dusty bed
I could not bear the life down there
With earth worms creeping through my hair
AARON S. BURBANK, WINSTEAD, CONNECTICTUT

❧

Robert Lives Esq.
A Barrister
So great a lover of peace
That when a contention arose
Between life & Death
He immediately gave up the
ghost to end the dispute.
ROBERT LIVES, RICHMOND,
VIRGINIA, AUGUST 12, 1819

THREE

INSULT
THY
NEIGHBOR

*Make sure to be nice to your loved ones
and neighbors, since you never know who
will be writing your epitaph.*

Here lies one who lived unloved, and died unlamented;
Who denied plenty to himself, assistance to his friends,
And relief to the poor;
Who starved his family, oppressed his neighbours, and
Plagued himself to gain what he
Could not enjoy;
At last, Death, more merciful to him than he was to himself
Released him from care, and his family from want;
And here he lies with the unknown he imitated, and with the
Soil he loved,
In fear of resurrection,
Lest his heirs should have spent the money he left behind,
Having laid up no treasure where moth and rust do not
Corrupt and thieves break through and steal.
Anonymous, Melmerby Parish Church,
Cumberland, England

☾

To the memory of Susan Mum:
Silence is wisdom.
Susan Mum, Nelson Parish Church,
Burnley, Lancashire, England

🦢

This stone was raised by Sarah's Ford
Not Sarah's virture to record
For they're well-known to all the town
But it was raised to keep her down.
Sarah Ford, Kilmurry Churchyard, Scotland

🐦

Here lies the clay of
Mitchell Coots,
Whose feet yet occupy his boots.
His soul has gone—we know not where
It landed, neither do we care.
Mitchell Boots, somewhere in Colorado

Here lies John Hill
A man of skill
Whose age was five times ten:
He never did good
And never would
If he lived as long again
John Hill, Bishop Auckland, Durham, England

Here lies John Rackett
In his wooden jacket
He kept neither horses nor mules;
He lived like a hog
And died like a dog
And left all his money to fools.
John Rackett, location unknown

This is the last resting place
Of dear Jemimer's bones
Her soul ascended into space
Amidst our tears and groans
She was not pleasing to the eye
Nor had she any brain
And when she talked was through her nose
Which gave her friends much pain
But still we feel she's worth
The money that was spent
Upon the coffin and the hearse
(The mourning plumes were lent.)
Anonymous

He meant well
Tried a little
Failed much
David Goodman Croly, location unknown

Milk and water sold I ever
Weight and measure gave I never,
So to the devil I must go,
woe, woe, woe, woe.
ANONYMOUS, EARLS BARTON CEMETERY,
NORTHAMPTONSHIRE, ENGLAND

◆

At rest beneath this slab of stone
Lies stingy Jimmy Wyatt
He died one morning just at ten
And saved a dinner by it
JIMMY WYATT, FALKIRK, ENGLAND

~

Here lies poor Ned Pardon
From misery free,
Who long was a bookseller's hack;
He led such a damnable life
In this world
I don't think he'll ever wish to come back.
EDWARD PARDON, ST. BRIDE'S CHURCH,
LONDON, ENGLAND

☾

Dear drunk old SUSAN oft was found;
But now she's laid beneath the ground,
Alas door-nail dead—alas the day!
Her nose was red, and moist as clay.
From morn to night, of care bereft,
She plied her glass, and wet her throttle,
Without a sigh her friends she left
But much she grieved to leave her bottle.
ANONYMOUS, CROWCOMBE CEMETERY,
SOMERSET, ENGLAND

My father and mother were both insane
I inherited the terrible stain
My grandfather, grandmother, aunts and uncles
Were lunatics all, and yet died of carbuncles
ANONYMOUS, SOMEWHERE IN MARYLAND

❧

Here lies the body of a girl who died
Nobody mourned, nobody cried
How she lived and how she fared
Nobody knew and nobody cared
GUSSIE, OCANTO, WISCONSIN

❧

Here lies one who for medicine
Would not give a little gold
And so his life he lost:
I fancy now he'd wish to live
Again could he but guess
How much his funeral cost
ANONYMOUS, LOCATION UNKNOWN

∼

Unknown man shot in
The Jennison & Gallup Co.'s store
While in the act of burglaring
The safe on Oct. 13, 1905
(stone bought with money found on his person).
ANONYMOUS, SHELDON, VERMONT

☾

Here lies, Thank God, a woman who
Quarreled and stormed her whole life through;
Tread softly o'er her mouldering form
Or else you'll raise another storm.
ANONYMOUS

Dead drunk, here Elderton, doth lie
Dead as he is, he still is dry;
So of him it may well be said,
Here is he, but not his thirst, is laid
WILLIAM ELDERTON,
LOCATION UNKNOWN

❧

All flesh is grass
The scriptures do say
And grass when dead
Is turned to hay
Now when the reaper her away do take
What a whopping haystack she will make
ANONYMOUS

❧

Another that banks on the same joke, sort of:

Beneath the gravel and these stones,
Lies poor Jack Tiffey's skin and bones,
His flesh I oft heard him say,
He hoped in time would make good hay;
Quoth I, "How can that come to pass?"
And he replied, "All flesh is grass."
JACK TIFFEY, PICKERING CEMETERY,
YORKSHIRE, ENGLAND

~

Hurrah! My boys at the Parson's fall
For if he'd lived he'd a'buried us all
ANONYMOUS, TAIBACH CHURCHYARD,
SOUTH WALES

Here lies John Moore, a miser old
Who filled his cellar with silver and gold.
Oh more, he cried, Old Moore, Old Moore,
'Twas clear he would not close the door,
and yet he cried, oh more, Old More.
Anonymous, Yarmouth Cemetery,
Isle of Wight

☾

Here lies the body of our Jean
None in the parish half so mean
She stayed in bed her clothes to save
And nearly drowned to save a grave
When we all rise on judgment day
She'll lie here still
If there's aught to pay.
Anonymous

❦

Here lies a miser who lived for himself
Who cared for nothing but gathering wealth
Now where he is and how he fared
Nobody knows and nobody cares.
Anonymous, Lemmington, England

❧

Floyd died and few have sobbed
Since he had lived all had been robbed
He's paid Dame Nature's debt 'tis said
The only one he ever paid
Some doubt that he resigned his breath
Some vow he's even cheated death
If he is buried, then ye Dead, beware
Look to your swaddlings, of your shrouds take care
Lest Floyd to your coffin should make his way
And steal your linen from your mouldering clay.
Anonymous

Stop passenger for here is laid
One who the debt of nature paid.
This is not strange, the reader cries,
We all know here a dead man lies.
You're right; but stop, I'll tell you more:
He never paid a debt before;
And now he's gone, I'll further say
He never will another pay.
ANONYMOUS, CORBRIDGE CEMETERY,
NORTHUMBERLAND, ENGLAND

Here lies Ned
There is nothing more to be said
Because we like to speak well of the dead.
ANONYMOUS

In memory of Beza. Wood
Departed this life
Nov. 2, 1837
Aged 45 years
Here lies one Wood
Enclosed in wood
One Wood within another
The outer wood is very good
We cannot praise the other
BEZA. WOOD, WINSLOW, MAINE 1837

Stranger rejoice:
This tomb holds
Arabella Young
Who on May 5, 1837
Began to hold her tongue
ARABELLA YOUNG, CHESTER PARISH CHURCH,
CHESHIRE, ENGLAND

Here's a variation:

Here lies, returned to clay
Miss Arabella Young
Who on the 1 of May, 1771
Began to hold her tongue
DOWNAL, VERMONT, OR MAYBE HATFIELD, MASSACHUSETTS

And yet another variation:

Underneath this sod lies ARABELLA YOUNG,
Who on the 5th of May began to hold her tongue.

Might this be the inspiration for Arabella's tomb?:

Here lyes Margaret Young,
Who had she lived
Would surely be hung
By the length of her tongue.

❧

Those who knew him best deplored him most
JOHN YOUNG, ST. ANDREW'S, STATEN ISLAND, NEW YORK

〜

Thin in beard and thick in purse
Never man beloved worse
He went to the grave
With many a curse
The devil and he had both
One nurse
ANONYMOUS

☾

If Heaven be pleased when sinners cease to sin
If Hell be pleased when sinners enter in
If Earth be pleased when ridded of a knave
Then all be pleased for Coleman's in his grave.
ANONYMOUS

Here is my much loved Celia laid
At rest for all her earthly labors
Glory to God! Peace to the Dead!
And the ease of all her neighbors
ANONYMOUS

❧

Here lies John Bairf in the
Only place for which he never applied
JOHN BAIRF, LOCATION UNKNOWN

❧

He faults are buried
With him beneath this stone
His virtues (if he had any)
Are remembered by his friends
ASA BARTON, NORWAY, MAINE

P.S.
The Old Nuisance
PHILIP SYNDEY BENNETT,
EAST CALAIS, VERMONT

~

Another one that has several versions and is, therefore, unfortunately suspect:

Mary Anne has gone to rest
Safe at last on Abraham's breast
Which may be nice for Mary Anne
But it's certainly rough on Abraham.

Here's a variation:

Eliza Ann
Has gone to rest
She now reclines on
Abraham's breast:
Peace at last for Eliza Ann
But not for Father Abraham

Beneath this stone and not above it
Lie the remains of Anna Lovett
Be pleased, dear reader, not to shove it
Lest she should care to come above it
For twixt you and I, no one does covet
To see again this Anna Lovett.
ANNA LOVETT,
LOCATION UNKNOWN, 1720

☾

Beneath this cold stone
Lies a son of the Earth
His story is short
Though we date from his birth
His mind was gross
His body was big
He drank like a fish
And he ate like a pig
No cares of religion
Of wedlock or state
Did e'er for a moment
Encumber John's pate
He sat or he walked
But his walk was creeping
Without foe, without friend
Unnotic'd he died
Not a single soul laughed
Not a single soul cried
Like his four-footed namesake
He dearly loved Earth
So the sexton has covered
His body with turf
JOHN MOLE, WORCESTER,
ENGLAND, 1756

Here lies Pecos Bill
He always lied
He always will
He once lied loud
Now he lies still.
PECOS BILL, GRAND FORKS,
NORTH DAKOTA

❧

Poems and epitaphs are but stuff;
Here lies Robert Burrows, that is enough
ROBERT BURROWS,
BEDLINGTON CHURCHYARD,
DURHAM, ENGLAND

❧

She lived—what more can there be said
She died—and all we know she's dead.
MARY HOYT, BRADFORD,
VERMONT, 1836

❧

Here lies an editor!
Snooks if you will;
In mercy, kind Providence, let him lie still!
He lied for a living; so
He lived while he lied:
When he could lie no longer
He lied down and died.
ANONYMOUS

Here continueth to rot
The body of Frances Chartres;
Who with an inflexible constancy
And inimitable uniformity of life
Persisted
In spite of Age & Infirmities,
In the practice of every Human vice,
Excepting Prodigality & Hypocrisy;
His insatiable Avarice exempted him from the first,
His matchless Impudence from the second.
Nor was he more singular in the undeviating pravity
Of his manners, than successful in accumulating
Wealth
For without Trade or Profession,
Without Trust of Public Money,
And without Bribe-Worthy Service,
He acquired, or more properly created
A Ministerial Estate
He was the only person of his time
Who could cheat without the mask of honesty;
Retain his primeval Meanness when possessed of
Ten Thousand a Year;
And, having daily deserving the Gibbet for what he did,
Was at last condemned to it for what he could not do.
O indignant reader!
Think not his life useless to mankind
Providence connived at his execrable designs.
To give to after the ages a conspicuous Proof and
Example
Of how small estimation is exorbitant wealth in
The sight of God
By his bestowing it all on the most unworthy of
ALL MORTALS.
FRANCES CHARTRES,
CHRIST'S CHURCHYARD,
SOUTHGATE, ENGLAND

Here lyeth hee, that lyed in ev'ry page;
The scorn of men, dishonour of his age;
Parliament's Pander, & ye nation's cheat;
Ye kingdom's jugler, impudency's seat;
The armye's spanyill, and ye gen'ralls witch;
Ye divell's godson, grandchild of a bitch;
Clery's blasphemer, enemy to ye king;
Under yis dunghill lyes a filthy ying;
Lilly, ye wise-men's hate, fooles adoration
Lilly, ye infamy of the English nation.
William Lilly, St. Margaret's,
Westminster, England, 1681

⁓

Here fast asleep lies Saunders Scott,
Long may he snort and snore;
His bains are now in Gorman's pot,
That used to strut the streets before.
He lived a lude and tastrel life,
For gude he nae regarded;
His perjur'd clack rais'd mickle strife,
For whilk belike he'll be rewarded.
Unverified

☾

Pity, not envy, be the lot
Of him who lieth here! I wot
A thousand deaths he long endured
Until his ills were cured.
Stranger, pass on, and make no riot—
Take care he slumbers on the quiet,
Nor break the only sleep (tis true)
Unhappy Scarron ever knew.
Scarron, Liverpool, England

Afterthought, and desecration, on the tomb of Thomas Jay, a Justice of the Peace, by one who must have held a grudge:

Here lieth Sir Thomas Jay, Knight,
Who, being dead, I upon his grave did shite.
POOLE, DORSET, ENGLAND

❧

Some of the best epitaphs are not written in stone, but in honor (or dishonor), of a loved or hated individual by a prominent poet or writer of the day, a practice that was well known in the 18th century. The best of these were written by Robert Burns, the national bard of Scotland. Here is a sampling of his best:

Here lyes with Dethe auld
Grizzel Grimme
Lincludens ugly wiche:
O Dethe, an' what a taste hast thou
Cann lye with sich a bitche!

Here cursing, swearing Burton lies,
A buck, a beau, or "dem my eyes!'
Who in this life did little good,
His last words were "dem my blood!"

Here lies Boghead among the dead,
In hopes to get salvation
But if such as he in Heav'n may be
Then welcome, Hail! Damnation.
LAIRD JAMES GRIEVE OF BOGHEAD,
TARBOLTON

❧

Here Souter Hood in death does sleep;
To Hell if he's gane thither,
Satan, gie him they gear to keep;
He'll haud it well the gither.
WILLIAM HOOD

As father Adam first was fool'd
(a case that's still too common)
Here lies a man woman ruled
The Devil ruled the woman
Oh Death, hadst thou but spared his life
Whom this day we did lament
We freely wad exchange the wife
And a'been well content.
E'en as he is, cauld in his graff,
The swoop we yet will do't;
Take thou the carlins carcass off,
Thou'se get the saul o'boot.
One Queen Artemisia, as old stories tell
When deprived of her husband she loved so well
In respect for the love and affection he showed her
She reduced him to dust and she drank up the powder
But Queen Netherplace, of a different complexion
When called on the order the funeral direction
Would have eat her dead lord, on a slender pretence,
Not to show her respect, but to save the expense.
LAIRD WILLIAM CAMPBELL OF NETHERPLACE

∼

Below thir stanes lie Jamie's bones;
O Death, it's my opinion
Thou ne'er took such a blth'ran bitch
Into thy dark dominion.
Humphrey James
Sic a reptile was wat,
Sic a miscreant slave,
That the worms ev'n damned him
When laid in his grave;
'In his skull there's famine,'
A starved reptile cries,
'And his heart is rank poison!'
Another replies.
WALTER RIDDLE

Here lies a mock marquis
Whose titles were shamm'd
If ever he rise, it will be to be damned.

☾

Hic Jacit (here lies) wee Johnnie
Whoe'er thou art, O reader, know,
That Death has murder'd Johnnie;
An' here his body lies fu'lowe,
Four saul he ne'er had any.
John Wilson

❧

Lament him, Mauchline husbands a',
He aften did assist ye;
For had ye staid hale weeks away,
Your wives they ne'er had miss'd ye.

❧

Ye Mauchline bairns, as on ye press
To school in bands thegither,
O tread ye lightly on his grass,–
Perhaps he was your father!
James Smith

〜

Here lie Willie Michie's bones
Oh Satan, when ye take him
Gie him the schulin of your weans
For clever deils he'll make them
William Michie,
Schoolmaster, Fifeshire

Ye maggots, feed on Nicol's brain,
For few sic feasts you've gotten;
And fix your claws in Nicol's heart,
For deil a bit o't's rotten.
WILLIAM NICOL, HIGH SCHOOL, EDINBURGH

☾

Another poet, George Gordon Noel (Lord Bryon), who wrote in the 19th century, offers this little gem, dedicated to Lord Castlereagh, the much disliked Foreign Secretary and Leader of the House of Commons, who committed suicide in 1822:

Posterity will ne'er survey
A nobler grave than this.
Here lie the bones of
Castlereagh
Stop, traveler, and piss.

This one was proposed by the poet himself:

This Grave contains all
that was Mortal of a
YOUNG ENGLISH POET
Who on his Death Bed,
In the Bitterness of his heart
At the malicious power of his enemies,
Desired these Words to be engraved
On his tombstone:
Here lies one
Whose name was writ in water.
JOHN KEATS, DIED 1821

Another proposed epitaph was written for Tom Purdie, who was servant to Sir Walter Scott. It seems that Mr. Purdie had a penchant for imbibing alcohol that didn't belong to him. Hence, Sir Walter proposed the following:

Here lies one who might have been trusted with untold gold,
But not with unmeasured whiskey.

Columnist for the Baltimore Sun, *and author of* The American Language, *H. L. Mencken, suggested an epitaph for himself: "If, after I depart this vale, you remember me and have some thought to please my ghost, forgive some sinner and wink at some homely girl." His last words were reportedly, "Remember me to my friends, tell them I'm a Hell of a mess."*

❧

Her temper furious
Her tongue was vindictive
She resented a look
And frowned at a smile
And was sour as vinegar
She punished the earth
Upwards of 40 years
To say nothing of her relations.
ANONYMOUS, MASSACHUSETTS

FOUR

TSK
TSK

What a place to make a mistake! These epitaphs are not intentionally amusing, but they are funny nonetheless. In some it's simply a spelling error, in others it's a strange turn of phrase that makes us wonder, did they really mean to say THAT?

In memory of
Major John Sewall
An architect of the first class
From whose fabrications great benefits
Have resulted to society;
He was benevolent, hospitable, and
Generous, without ostentation
And pious without enthusiasm.
He died July 23rd, 1818. Aet. 91
York, Maine

☾

Lord, She is Thin
Susannah Ensign, Cooperstown,
New York, 1825

🐌

Once I was alive
And had flesh, did thrive
But now I am a skellitant at 70.
Sunnigdale Church,
Berkshire, England

❧

Mary E. Wife of Benjamin Lee Craft
And daughter of Bridges and Sarah
Arendell who was born Jan. 1, 1825
And died Sept. 4th, 1858
Tho' he slay me yet will I trust in him.
Mary E. Craft, Beaufort,
North Carolina

Here lieth
The body
Of
John Rees
Who departed this life
Octr the 17th, 1824
Aged 249 years
Reader prepare to meet thy God. [*just not so soon*]
John Rees, Amroth, Pembrokeshire, England

~

Sacred to the memory
Of our 'steamed friend.
Anonymous

☾

Here lies a virgin,
with her babe
resting in her arms.
Anonymous, Snow Camp, North Carolina

❦

Upon the fifth day of November
Christ's College lost a privy member;
Cupid and Death did both their arrows nick,
Cupid shot short, but death did hit the prick;
Women lament and maidens make great moans,
Because the prick is laid beneath the stones.
A man with the unfortunate name of Pricke,
somewhere in England.

❧

Here lyes JOHN and MARY his bride,
They lived and they laugh'd while they were able,
And at last were obliged to knock under the table.
Anonymous, Harrogate Cemetery,
Yorkshire, England

He was literally a father to all the
Children of the parish.
Anonymous

~

Here lies JEMMY LITTLE, a carpenter industrious
A very good-natured man, but somewhat blusterous.
When that his little wife his authority withstood
He took a little stick and banged her as he would.
His wife now left alone, her loss does so deplore,
She wishes Jemmy back to bang her a little more;
For now he's dead and gone this fault appears so small,
A little thing would make her think it was no fault at all.
Anonymous, Portsmouth Cemetery,
Hampshire, England

☾

Brigham Young
Born
On this spot
1801
A man of much
Courage
And superb equipment.
Brigham Young, yes
THE Brigham Young, Utah

✿

Daniel Chappell who was killed in
The act of taking a whale, October 18, 1845, aged 25 years
Blessed are the dead that die in the Lord
Montville, Connecticut

Here lies inter'd
The mortal remains
Of John Hulm
Printer
Who, like an old, worn-out type
Battered by frequent use
Reposes in the grave
But not without a hope
That at some future time
He might be cast in the mold
Of righteousness
And safely locked up
In the chase of immortality
He was distributed from
The board of life
On the 9th day of Sept. 1827
Aged 75
Regretted by his employers
And respected by his fellow artists.
JOHN HULM, ST. MICHAEL'S CHURCH, COVENTRY, ENGLAND

This is very similar to Benjamin Franklin's proposed epitaph for himself. Although his actual gravestone simply has his name and the name of his wife, what he wrote for himself read:

The body of Benjamin Franklin/Printer/(Like the cover of an old book its contents torn out/and stript of its lettering and gilding)/ Lies here, food for worms/ But the work itself / shall not be lost/ For it will, as he believed/ appear once more/ In a new/ and more elegant edition/ Revised and corrected/ By/ The Author. [*Ben, unlike poor John, was not regretted by his employer*].

❧

Here lies the body of Mrs. Annie Smith
Who departed this life Octo. The 28th,
in the year 1701
She lived a maid and died aged 708.
ANNIE SMITH, BICKENHILL CHURCHYARD, ENGLAND

Sacred to twins Charlie and Varlie
Sons of loving parents who died in infancy
Anonymous

~

Here lies one who never sacrificed
His reason at the altar of
Superstitions God, who never
Believed Jonah swallowed the whale.
Jonathan Richardson,
East Thompson, Connecticut

☾

Here lies poor William Jones
Who all his life collected bones;
But death, that great and grisly spectre,
That most amazing bone collector
Hath boned poor Jones, so neat & tidy
That here he lies in bona-fide.
Alston, Cumberland, England;
also reported at St. Lawrence's Church,
on the Isle of Wight

🐌

Travellers
I will relate a prodigy
On the day whereon the
Aforesaid Thomas Carter
Breathed out his soule
A Sudbury camel passed
Through the eye of a needle
GO—and if thou art wealthy
Do likewise.
Thomas Carter,
Sudbury, Suffolk, England

Here lies the dust of Louisa Orr
Whose soul is now a little angle in Heaven.
Germantown, Pennsylvania

*Another tombstone in Elon College, North Carolina bears
the same mistake:*

Our Little Darling has gone to be an angle.

❧

Ira Prentice
Deceased July 20, 1819
in ye 9th year of his age
He lived a life of virtue
And died of the cholera morbis
Caused by eating green fruit
In the certain hope of a blessed immortality.
Go reader, and do likewise.
Ira Prentice, Burlington,
Massachusetts

～

Here lies the body of James Vernon
Only surviving son of Admiral Vernon
Also reported as Thomas Vernon
in Plymouth, Massachusetts

☾

Here lies father, and mother, and sister and I
We all died within the space of one short year
They were all buried at Wimble except I
And I be buried here
Anonymous, Nettlebed Churchyard,
Oxfordshire, England

Here lies John Higley, whose father
And mother drowned in their passage from America
Had they lived, they would have been buried here.
JOHN HIGLEY, BELTURBET, IRELAND

❧

Stranger Pause
And shed a tear
For Mary Jane
lies buried here
Mingled in a
most surprising manner
With Susan, Joy
and parts of Hannah.
ANONYMOUS

❧

Here lies the bones of foolish Fred
Who wasted precious time in bed
A fellow hit him on the head
And thanks be praised—our Freddie's dead.
ANONYMOUS

~

Here lies the wife of Robert Ricular
Who walked the way of God
Perpendicular
ANONYMOUS

Was she a straight-laced upstanding woman, or one who refused to join her husband in the matrimonial bed?

☾

To the short memory
Of Marvin Trueham
Regretted by all who never knew him.
MARVIN TRUEHAM, LOCATION UNKNOWN

Underneath this stone
Lies poor John Round
Lost at sea
And never found
REPORTED AT MARBLEHEAD, NORFOLK,
SOMEWHERE IN IRELAND, AND MARPLE, DERBYSHIRE, ENGLAND.
OCCASIONALLY, THE NAME IS GIVEN AS JONATHAN GROUND.

❧

Here lies old
Aunt Hannah Proctor
Who purged but didn't
call the doctor
She couldn't stay
She had to go
Praise be to God, from whom
All blessings flow.
HANNAH PROCTOR, QUEENSBOROUGH CEMETERY,
MEDWAY, KENT, ENGLAND

❧

Faithful husband, thou art
At rest until we meet again.
EDWARD OAKES, WEST CEMETERY,
MIDDLEBURY, VERMONT, 1866

∼

Here lies Peter Montgomery,
Who was accidentally shot in his thirtieth year
This monument was erected by grateful relatives.
PETER MONTGOMERY,
LOCATION UNKNOWN

Erected to the memory of
John MacFarlane
Drowned in the water of Leith
By a few affectionate friends
JOHN MACFARLANE, EDINBURGH, SCOTLAND

With friends like these . . .

☾

Richard Kendrick
Was buried August 29, 1785
By the desire of his wife
Margaret Kendrick
RICHARD KENDRICK,
WREXHAM CHURCHYARD, ENGLAND

This gives new meaning to "till death do us part."

❧

My glass is rum.
JAMES EWINS, FOREST HILL CEMETERY,
EAST DERRY, NEW HAMPSHIRE, 1781

❧

To the memory of
MAJOR JAMES BRUSH
Who was killed by the accidental
discharge of a pistol by his orderly
14 April 1831
Well done good and faithful servant.
JAMES BRUSH, WOOLWICH CHURCHYARD,
ENGLAND, 1831

To the memory of Abraham Beaulieu
Born 15 Sept, 1822
Accidentally shot
April 1844
As a mark of affection
From his brother.
Sleeps in peace after life's fitful fever
ABRAHAM BEAULIEU, LA POINTE, WISCONSIN. ANOTHER IS
REPORTED TO READ THE SAME, UNDER THE NAME JOHN PHILLIPS
IN FINCHLEY CEMETERY, LONDON, ENGLAND AND ULSTER, IRELAND

Sacred to the memory of three twins.
ANONYMOUS

Here lieth
John James
The old Cook
Of Newby
Who was a faithful
Servant
To his master
And an
Upright downright
Honest man.
Banes among stanes
Do lie sou still,
Whilk the soul wanders
E'en where God will.
JOHN JAMES, RIPON CATHEDRAL,
YORKSHIRE, ENGLAND, 1760.

Let her RIP.
ANONYMOUS

Let's save some space, shall we?:

MS
To the pious memory
of
Ralph Quelche and Jane his wife

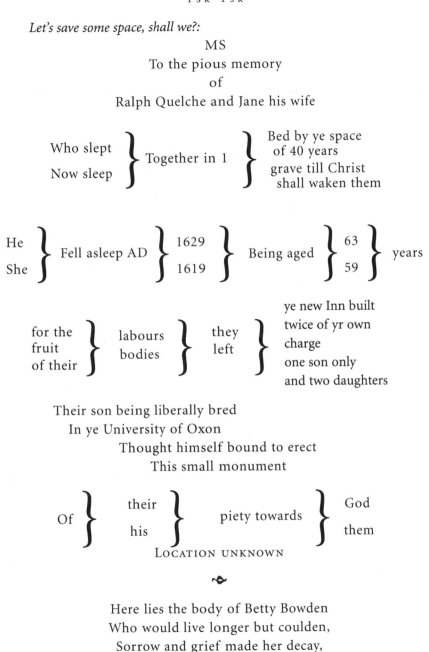

Who slept } Together in 1 } Bed by ye space
Now sleep } of 40 years
grave till Christ
shall waken them

He } Fell asleep AD } 1629 } Being aged } 63 } years
She } 1619 } 59

for the } labours } they } ye new Inn built
fruit } bodies } left } twice of yr own
of their charge
one son only
and two daughters

Their son being liberally bred
In ye University of Oxon
Thought himself bound to erect
This small monument

Of } their } piety towards } God
his } them

LOCATION UNKNOWN

Here lies the body of Betty Bowden
Who would live longer but coulden,
Sorrow and grief made her decay,
Till her bad leg card her away.
BETTY BOWDEN, STAVERTON, ENGLAND

FIVE

HAPPILY EVER AFTER

*The hopes and dreams of newlywed
couples include a life free from strife.
Sadly, sometimes those dreams just don't
come true. In these epitaphs you will see
a boiling resentment that endures long
after death doth part.*

To free me from domestic strife,
Death call'd at my house, but he spoke with my wife.
Susan, wife of David Pattison, lies buried here
Oct. 19, 1706.
Stop reader, and if not in a hurry, shed a tear.

'Cause it doesn't sound like David's gonna do it.

Susan Pattison, Suffolk, England

☾

Would that I could be remembered for being such a good wife!
She looked well after the hogs, the chickens,
And cows, and always kept my socks darned.
Anonymous, Granary Burying Ground,
Boston, Massachusetts

❧

Here lies the body of Manny
They put him here to stay:
He lived the life of Riley
While Riley was away.
Anonymous, unverifiable

❧

Here lies John and likewise Mary
Cheek by jowl and never weary;
No wonder they so well agree,
John wants no punch, nor Moll no tea.
John Collier & Mary, Rochdale Cemetery, England

～

Elizabeth McFadden
Wife of David P. Reid
Died Feb. 28, 1859
In her 47th year
She never done one thing to displease her husband
Silver Lake, New York

God be praised;
Here is Mr. Dudley senior,
And Jane his wife also,
Who, while living, was his superior,
But see what death can do.
ANONYMOUS, BROOM PARISH CHURCHYARD,
WORCESTERSHIRE, ENGLAND

☽

One of the best mother-in-laws
God ever made
ANONYMOUS, HAMILTON, OHIO

❧

Here lies John's wife, plague of his life;
She spent his wealth, she harmed his health;
And she left him daughters three, just as bad as she.
ANONYMOUS

❧

Here lies the quintessence
Of noise and strife,
Or, in one word,
Here lies a scolding wife;
Had not Death took her
When her mouth was shut,
He durst not for his ears
Have touch'd the slut.
ANONYMOUS, LOCATION UNKNOWN

～

Great was my grief, I could not rest
God called me hence—thought it best;
Unhappy marriage was my fate,
I did repent when it was too late.
ST. ALBAN'S CEMETERY,
HERTFORDSHIRE, ENGLAND

Here lyes a man, who all his mortal life
Passed mending clocks, but could not mend his wife.
The 'larum of his bell was ne'er sae shrill
As was her tongue, aye clacking like a mill.
But now he's gone,—oh, whither, nane can tell,
I hope beyond the sound of Mally's bell.
ANONYMOUS, HODDAM, DUMFRIESHIRE, ENGLAND

☾

Three of her husbands slumber here.
This turf has drunk a widow's tear.
ANONYMOUS, BARTON UNDER NEEDWOOD CHURCH,
STAFFORDSHIRE, ENGLAND

❧

Here lies Ephram Wise
Between his two wives
One was Tilly
One was Sue
Both were faithful, loyal and true
But I hope that my friends from Adam to Willy
Will lay me down so I'm tilting towards Tilly
EPHRAM WISE, REPORTEDLY IN TAOS, NEW MEXICO

❧

Oh cruel Death! why wert thou so unkind,
To take the one, and leave the other behind?
Thou should'st have taken both or neither,
Which would have been more agreeable to the survivor.
ANONYMOUS, BIRMINGHAM, WARWICKSHIRE, ENGLAND

∼

Farewell, dear wife! My life is past;
I loved you while my life did last;
Don't grieve for me, or sorrow take
But love my brother, for my sake.
ANONYMOUS, SARATOGA, NEW YORK

Here lies the body of Captain Tully,
Aged a hundred and nine years fully;
And threescore years before, as Mayor,
The sword of this city he did bear;
Nine of his wives do with him lie,
so shall the tenth when she die.

CAPTAIN TULLY, EXETER CATHEDRAL, ENGLAND

☾

Here lies my wife, a sad slattern and shrew,
If I said I regretted her, I should lie too!

ANONYMOUS, SELBY, YORKSHIRE, ENGLAND

A variation:

Here lies Polly, a terrible shrew;
If I said I was sorry, I should lie too.

✶

My dear and beloved wife
Thou has left me to mourn thy loss
And by the blessings of God & Son
I have found another wife.

ANONYMOUS

↬

MARSHALL

He	Willie	She
Never	1872–1944	Always
Did	his wife	Did
	Della Longe	Her
	1876	Best

WILLIE AND DELLA LONGE MARSHALL
HARDWICK, VERMONT

In memory of
Charles Ward
Who died May 1770
Aged 63 years
A dutiful son
A loving brother
And
An affectionate husband
NO this stone was not
Erected by Susan, his wife
She erected a stone to
John Salter, her second husband
Forgetting the affection of
Charles Ward, her fyrst husband

CHARLES WARD, LOWESTOFT, ENGLAND

❧

Here lies my wife in earthly mold
Who when she lived did not but scold
Peace, wake her not, for now she's still,
She had, but now I have my will

ANON, ELLON CHURCHYARD

Here's a variation:

Here lies my wife
In earthly mould
Who when she lived
Did naught but scold:
Good friends go softly
In your walking here
Lest she should wake
And rise up talking

REPORTED IN BEDFORD, TROUTBECK, WESTMORELAND
AND PONTELAND, NORTHUMBERLAND, ENGLAND

In memory of
Elizabeth who
Should have been the
Wife of Mr.
Simeon Palmer
Who died augt 14th
1776 in the 64th year
of her age

In memory of
Lidia ye wife of
Mr. Simeon Palmer
who died December
26th 1754 in ye 35
year of her age

LIDIA PALMER AND ELIZABETH ANON., LITTLE COMPTON, RHODE ISLAND

Here lies the bodies of Thomas Bond and Mary his wife
She was temperate, chaste and charitable BUT
She was proud, peevish and passionate. She was
An affectionate wife, and a tender mother BUT
Her husband and her child whom she loved
Seldom saw her countenance without a disgusting frown,
Whilst she received visitors who she despised with an endearing smile
Her behavior was discreet towards strangers
BUT Independent to her family, Abroad her conduct
Was influenced by good breeding BUT
At home, by ill temper. She was a professed enemy
To flattery, and was seldom known to praise or command
BUT the talents which she principally excelled were
Difference of opinion and discovering flaws
And imperfections BUT she was an admirable economist
And, with prodigality dispensed plenty to every person
In her family: BUT would sacrifice their eyes to a farthing candle
She sometimes made her husband glad with her good qualities
BUT much more made him frequently miserable with her many failings
Insomuch that in 30 years cohabitation
He often lamented all her virtues
He had not in the whole enjoyed two years of matrimonial comfort
BUT at length finding that she had lost the affection of her husband
As well as the regard of her neighbors
Family disputes having been divulged by servants
She died of vexation, July 20, 1768, aged 48 years
BUT her worn-out husband survived her four months and two day
And departed this life Nov. 28, 1768
In the 54th year of his age
FURTHER
William Bond, brother to the deceased erected this stone
As a weekly monitor to the surviving wives of this parish
That they may avoid the infamy of having their memories
Handed to posterity with a patchwork character.
THOMAS AND MARY BOND, HORSLEY DOWN CHURCH,
CUMBERLAND, ENGLAND

When dear papa went up to Heaven
What grief mama endured
And yet that grief was softened
For papa was insured
ANONYMOUS

☾

Father   Mother
Divided in Life—United in Death
WOODLAWN CEMETERY,
PHILADELPHIA, PENNSYLVANIA

❦

Here let a bard unenvied rest
Whom no dull critic dare molest
Escaped from the familiar ills
Of thread-bare coat and unpaid bills
From rough bum bailiffs upstart duns
From sneering pride's detested sons
From all those pes'tring ills of life
From, worst of all, a scolding wife
ANONYMOUS, HOUGHTON-ON-THE-HILL CHURCHYARD,
LEICESTERSHIRE, ENGLAND

❧

Sacred to the memory of Mr. Jared Bates
Who died August the 6th, 1800
His widow, aged 24,
who mourns as one who can be comforted
lives at 7 Elm Street
Has every good qualification of a good wife
JARED BATES,
LINCOLN, MAINE

Stay, bachelor, if you have wit
A wonder to behold
A husband and a wife in one dark pit
Lie close and never scold
Tread softy though for fear she wakes
Hark!—she begins already
You've hurt my head—my shoulder aches
These sots can ne'er move steady
As friend, with happy freedom blest
See how my hopes miscarried
Not death itself can give you rest
Unless you die unmarried.
ANONYMOUS, SHEFFIELD, ENGLAND

Resurgam! [I am Risen!]
But don't tell my husband of it.
ANONYMOUS

She was married twenty-six
Years and in all that time
Never once banged the door
ANONYMOUS

"Husband, prepare to follow me!"
I cannot come my dearest wife
For I have married another wife
And much as I would come to thee
I now must live and die with she

Another variation on this theme reads:

Grieve not for me, my husband dear
I am not dead but sleeping here
With patience wait, prepare to die
And in short time, you'll come to I
I am not grieved, my dearest wife
Sleep on, I've got another wife
Therefore I cannot come to thee
For I must go and sleep with she.
HEREFORD CHURCHYARD, ENGLAND

Here lies a woman
No man can deny it
She died in peace, although she lived unquiet
Her husband prays, if e'er this way you walk
You would tread softly—if she wake, she'll talk.
ANONYMOUS

❧

Here snug in her grave my wife doth lie,
Now she's at peace and so am I.
Or Here lies my wife: here let her lie,
Now she's at rest and so am I.
OLD GREY FRIARS CEMETERY,
EDINBURGH, SCOTLAND

〜

1890 The light of my life has gone out
1891 I have struck another match
ANONYMOUS

☾

Here lyes my poor wife
Without bed or blanket
But dead as any stone
God be thanket
ANONYMOUS, OXFORD, ENGLAND.

A variation is reported in Yorkshire; another rendition identifies the poor wife:
Here lies my wife EDIE,
Who in her time made me giddy:
Here she lies without bed or blanket,
As dead as a door-nail, the Lord be thanked.
TIDDINGTON CHURCH, OXFORD, ENGLAND

Here lies the body
of Mary Ford
We hope her soul
Is with the Lord
But if for Hell
She's changed this life
Better life there
Than as John Ford's wife
Mary Ford, Potterne, Wiltshire,
or maybe Upton-on-Severn, Worcestershire, England,
and again, maybe Tiddington Church, Oxford, England

❧

Warren Gibbs
Died by arsenic poisoning
March 23, 1860
Aged 36 years, 5 mo., 23 days
Think my friends when this you see
How my wife has done for me
She in some oysters did prepare
Some poison for my lot and fare
Then of some I did partake
And Nature yielded to its fate
Before she my wife became
Mary Felton was her name
Walter Gibbs, Knight's Corner,
Pelham, Massachusetts

❧

Here lies the body of James Robinson
And Ruth his wife
Their warfare is accomplished.
St. Saviour's Church, London, England

Also:

Wilbur Guttman
And his wife
Their warfare is accomplished.

And again:

Here lyeth Jas Ross
And Ruth his wife
They fought the good fight
Their warfare is accomplished
BRANCHPORT, NEW YORK

~

Here lies the body of   Here lies the bones
My lovely dear wife Anne   They call him Uncle Jim
Who plays the poker   he sits here and drinks
Machines whenever   while she puts his money
She can   in
JAMES THOMAS AND ANNE HEWITT, HELENSBURG CEMETERY,
NEW SOUTH WALES, AUSTRALIA

☾

This is to the memory of Ellen Hill
A woman who could always have her will
She snubbed her husband and she made good bread
Yet on the whole he's rather glad she's dead
She whipped her children and she drank her gin
Whipped virtue out and whipped the Devil in
May all such woman go to some great fold
Where they through all eternity may scold
ELLEN HILL, LOCATION UNKNOWN

❦

Who for breath this tomb does rest
Has joined the army of the blest
The Lord hath taken her to the sky
The Saints rejoice—and so do I.
ANN HUGHES, CHERENING-LE-CLAY, ENGLAND, 1750;
ALSO REPORTED IN THE SAME PLACE BUT THE FIRST LINE READS
A LITTLE DIFFERENTLY: WHO FAR BELOW THIS TOMB DOES REST

Here lies the man Richard
And Mary his wife
Whose surname was Pritchard
They lived without strife
And the reason was plain
They abounded in riches
They had no care or pain
And his wife wore the britches.
RICHARD AND MARY PRITCHARD, CHELMSFORD CATHEDRAL, ESSEX, ENGLAND

❧

Tears cannot restore her
Therefore I weep
ANONYMOUS

⌣

Sacred to the memory of Anthony Drake
Who died for peace and quiet's sake
His wife was constantly scolding and scoffin;
So he sought for repose in a twelve-dollar coffin
ANTHONY DRAKE, BURLINGTON CHURCHYARD, MASSACHUSETTS

☾

Under this marble tomb lies ye body of John Custis, esq.
Of the City of Williamsburg, and Parish of Bruton
Formerly of Hungar's Parish on the
Eastern Shore of Virginia and County of Northhampton
his place of nativity. Aged 71 years; and yet lived but seven years
which was the space of time of he kept a bachelor's house
At Arlington, on the Eastern shore of Virginia.
JOHN CUSTIS IV, CUSTIS PLANTATION, NORTHHAMPTON COUNTY, VIRGINIA 1749;
FATHER OF DANIEL PARK CUSTIS, WHO MARRIED A YOUNG MARTHA DANDRIDGE

*Two years after Daniel's death, Martha married one George
Washington (yes, father-of-the-United-States, George Washington).
We can only hope that Mary Ball Washington was a bit more lovable
than Martha's first mother-in-law.*

After having lived with her husband
Upwards of sixty-five years, she
Died in the hope of a
Resurrection to a better life
MRS. JOHN BROOKS, HILL BURYING GROUND,
CONCORD, MASSACHUSETTS

❦

Here's a variation:

She lived with her husband
Fifty years and died in the confident
Hope of a better life.
ANONYMOUS, BURLINGTON, VERMONT OR,
MAYBE, EASINGWOLD CHURCH, YORKSHIRE, ENGLAND

❧

Passing stranger, call it not
A place of fear and doom
I love to linger o'er this spot
It is my husband's tomb
MATTHIES BRANDEN, OLD MANDAN, BISMARCK, NORTH DAKOTA, 1882

Another is reported in England:

Stranger call this not
A place of gloom
To me it is a pleasant spot
My husband's tomb.
COCKERMOUTH, CUMBERLAND, ENGLAND

☾

Charity, wife of Gideon Bligh
Underneath this stone doth lie
Naught was she ever known to do
what her husband told her to.
CHARITY BLIGH, ST. MICHAEL PENKEVIL CHURCH,
DEVONSHIRE, ENGLAND, 1650

36-33-01-24-17
Honey you don't know what you did for me,
Always playing the lottery.
The numbers you picked came into play
Two days after you passed away
For this, a huge monument I do erect
For now I get a yearly check
How I wish you were alive,
For now we are worth 8.5
ELIZABETH RICH (APROPOS),
EUFAULA HISTORICAL CEMETERY,
EUFAULA, ALABAMA

❧

Here lies the body of Sarah Sexton
She was a wife that never vexed one
I can't say as much for the one
Underneath the next stone.
SARAH SEXTON & AN UNFORTUNATE SECOND WIFE,
FALKIRK, SCOTLAND

❧

The children of Israel wanted bread
And the Lord sent them manna.
Old Clerk Wallace wanted a wife
And the Devil sent him Anna.
ANNA WALLACE, RIBBESFORD, ENGLAND

❧

This spot's the sweetest
I've seen in my life
For it raises my flowers
And covers my wife
LLANELLY CEMETERY, WALES

Thomas Alleyn and his two wives
Death here advantage hath of life
I spye,
One husband with two wifes at once
May lie.
Thomas Alleyne,
Witchingham, England, 1650

☾

Seven wives I've buried
With may a fervent prayer
If we all should meet in Heaven
Won't there be trouble there?
Anonymous

✿

Here lies the wife of Brother Thomas
Whom tyrant death has torn from us,
Her husband never shed a tear
Until his wife was buried here
And then he made a fearful rout
For fear she might find her way out
Burlington, Vermont

ॐ

Here lies Cynthia, Steven's wife
She lived six years in calms and strife
Death came at last and set her free
I was glad and so was she
Hollis, New Hampshire

Sacred to the memory of
Elisha Philbrook and his wife Sarah
Within this grave do lie,
Back to back my wife and I
When the last trump the air shall fill
If she gets up I'll just lie still
SARGEANTVILLE, MAINE

In Memoriam
I plant these shrubs upon your grave, dear wife
That something on this spot may boast of life
Shrubs must wither and all earth must rot
Shrubs may revive: but you, thank Heaven, will not.
ANONYMOUS, RAYDONSHIRE, ENGLAND CIRCA 1899

A.D. 1827 I am anxiously awaiting you.
A.D. 1867 Here I am
ANONYMOUS, REPORTED IN PARIS, FRANCE

He that was sweet to my repose
Now is become stink under my nose
This is said of me
So it will be said of thee
DR. ISAAC BARTHOLOMEW, HILLSIDE CEMETERY,
CHESHIRE, CONNECTICUT, 1710

Beloved husband of Joan
A man with nature
Who loved his life & jigsaws
"didjabringabeer"
BRUCE ALEXANDER LINCOLN, SHOALHAVEN MEMORIAL GARDENS,
NEW SOUTH WALES, AUSTRALIA

Here lies Jane Smith
Wife of Thomas Smith
Marblecutter:
This monument erected
by her husband
as a tribute to her memory
monuments of this style
are 250 dollars
Jane Smith, Annapolis, Maryland

⁓

*Picture, if you will, three tombs in a row with carved hands upon
the stones depicting the direction in which the comment is directed.
The stone to the right points to the middle and reads in German:
Here rests my husband. The stone on the left points the other way,
again toward the middle stone and reads: He is mine too. The middle stone, with hand crossed and pointing at the two other stone
reads: These two are mine.*
Anonymous, Greenmount Cemetery, Baltimore, Maryland

☾

Above John Dale were in the 86th yeare of his
Pilgrimage, laid upon his two wives.
This thing in life might raise some jealousy,
Here all three together lovingly,
But from embraces here no pleasure flows,
Alike are here all human joys and woes;
Here Sarah's chiding John no longer hers,
And old John's rambling Sarah no more fears;
A period's come to all their toilsome lives,
The good man's quiet, still are both his wives.
Derbyshire, England

SIX

PURITY, PRURIENCE, & PROGENY

The subjects of these epitaphs were caught having sex, were so good at having sex that they spawned half the town, or are still, even in the grave, waiting to have sex.

Mary E. Oliver
Daughter of John & Elizabeth
Pearson Oliver. Died Mar. 6,
1836. Aged 82 years
Him that cometh to me I will in no wise cast out.
CEDAR GROVE CEMETERY,
NEW BERN, NORTH CAROLINA

☾

Here lies the body of barren PEG
Who had no issue but one in her leg;
But while she was living she was so cunning
That when one stood still the other was running.
ANONYMOUS, STANMORE CHURCHYARD,
MIDDLESEX, ENGLAND

❧

Here lies the body of one
Who died of constancy alone,
Stranger! Advance with steps courageous,
For this disease is not contagious.
ANONYMOUS, REPORTEDLY
FROM THE 19TH CENTURY

❧

Dorothy Cecil
Unmarried
As yet.
WIMBLEDON,
LONDON, ENGLAND

〜

Censure not rashly, though nature's apt to halt.
No woman's born that dies without a fault.
ST. MARY'S CHURCH,
ISLINGTON, LONDON, ENGLAND

Erected to the memory of Alexander Gray
Some time farmer in Mill of Burns, who
Died in the 96th year of his age, having
Had 32 legitimate children by two wives
ALEXANDER GRAY,
LOCATION UNKNOWN

☾

Here lies the body of Joan Carthew
Born at St. Columb; Died at St. Cue
Children she had five
Three dead and two alive
Those that are dead choosing rather
to die with their mother
Than live with their father
JOAN CARTHEW, ST. AGNES CHURCHYARD,
CORNWALL, ENGLAND

A variation on the same theme:

Here lies the mother of children seven
Three on earth and four in Heaven;
The four in Heaven preferring rather
To die with mother than live with father.
ANONYMOUS, GODOLPHIN CROSS CHURCH,
CORNWALL, ENGLAND

❧

Some have children
Some have none:
Here lies the
Mother of twenty-one
ANN JENNINGS, WOLSTANTON,
STAFFORDSHIRE, CHESHIRE, ENGLAND

Open, open wide ye Golden Gates
That lead to the Heavenly shore,
Our father suffered in his passing through
And mother weighs much more
Althea White, Lee, Massachusetts,
also given as Alpha White

❧

Here lies the body of Mary Ellis, Daughter of
Thomas Ellis and Lydia, his wife, of this parish.
She was a virgin of virtuous character, and most
Promising hopes. She died on the 3rd of June,
1609, aged one hundred and nineteen
Mary Ellis, Essex, England

～

Here lyes Bedal Willy Smyth,
Wha rang the auld kirk bell,
He buryed thousands in his day
And here he lyes himself;
Some say he was a married man,
Some say he was no,
But iv he ever had a spouse
She's no wi' him below
Bedal Willy Smythe,
St. Michael's Churchyard, Dumfries, England

☾

Five
Times he wived
But still survived
To seek a sixth he at
The age of 93 walked to
London but the journey got him down
Nicholas Toke, Kensington Cemetery,
London, England

Here lies Ann Mann
She lived an old maid
And died an old Mann
ANNE MANN, BATH ABBEY,
LONDON, ENGLAND, 1750

It is also reported as being in Barton Moss Cemetery, near Manchester, England.

❧

Of children in all she bore twenty-four
Thank the Lord there will be no more.
ANONYMOUS, CANTERBURY, ENGLAND

❧

Here lies the father of 29:
There would have been more
But he didn't have time
ANONYMOUS

∼

Here lies the good old knight SIR HARRY,
Who loved well, but would not marry.
ANONYMOUS,
DITCHLEY PARISH CHURCH,
OXFORDSHIRE, ENGLAND

☾

Beneath this silent stone is laid
A noisy, antiquated maid
Who from her cradle talked to death
And never before was out of breath.
ANONYMOUS, FALKIRK CEMETERY, SCOTLAND

'Tis true I led a single life
and ne'er was married in my life
for of that sex I ne'er had none
It is the Lord: His will be done

ANONYMOUS, BRAUNSTON CHURCHYARD,
NORTHAMPTONSHIRE, ENGLAND

❧

Here lies romantic PHOEBE,
Half Ganymede, half Hebe;
A Maid of mutable condition,
A jockey, cowherd and musician.

PHOEBE BROWN, MATLOCK,
DERBYSHIRE, ENGLAND

❧

Here lies the body
Of Mary Gwynne
Who was so very
Pure within
She cracked the shell
Of her earthly skin
And hatched herself
A cherubim

MARY GWYNNE, ST. ALBAN'S CHURCHYARD,
CAMBRIDGE, ENGLAND; THE NAME
IS ALSO GIVEN AS MARTHA

❧

Here lies the bones of
Elizabeth Charlotte
Born a virgin, died a harlot
She was aye a virgin at seventeen
A remarkable thing in Aberdeen

ELIZABETH CHARLOTTE, ABERDEEN, SCOTLAND

Also reported as:

Here lies the body
of Mabel Charlotte
Born a virgin
Died a harlot.
She was a virgin
Till her 21st year
A remarkable thing
In Oxfordshire

And again as:

Here lies poor Charlotte
Who was no harlot
But in her virginity
Though just turned nineteen—
Which within this vicinity
Is hard to be seen.
ANONYMOUS, REPORTEDLY IN WALES, UNVERIFIABLE

☾

Here lies the body of Martha Dias,
Who was always noisy, and not over pious;
She lived to the age of three score and ten
And gave that to the worms she refused
To the men
MARTHA DIAS, SHREWSBURY, SHROPSHIRE, ENGLAND, 1675.
A VARIATION HAS, "SHE WAS ALWAYS UNEASY."

🙚

Anne Harrison, well known as NANNA RAN DAN,
Who was chaste but no prude; & tho'
Free yet no harlot. By principle virtuous, by
Education a Protestant; her freedom made
Her liable to censure, while her extensive
Charities made her esteemed, but the rest of
her members she kept in subjection.
After a life of 80 years so lived, she died 1745.
ANNE HARRISON, EASINGWALD, ENGLAND

In memory of
Mrs. Lydia Burnett, who
Was first consort of Mr.
Noah Ripley, Esq.
By whom she had 8 sons & 11 daughters 17 of them lived to
Have families; her descendants at her death were 97
grandchildren & 106 greatgrandchildren
she died June 17th, 1816, Aged 91
Many daughters have done virtuously, but
Thou excellest.
LYDIA BURNETT, BUCKMINSTER CEMETERY,
BARRE, MASSACHUSETTS

Me thinks, Lydia excellest not enough—

❧

Here lieth the body
Of
Michael Honeywood
Who was grandchild and one
Of the three hundred and sixty-
Seven persons that Mary the
Wife of Robert Honeywood Esq.
Did see before she died, lawfully
Descended from her, viz. sixteen
Of her own body, 114 grandchildren
288 of the third generation and 9
of the fourth Mrs. Honeywood
died in the year 1605 in the
78th year of her age.
MICHAEL HONEYWOOD,
LOCATION UNKNOWN

Here lies the body of Mrs. Mary, wife of
Deacon John Buel, Esq. She died Nov. 4, 1768, aged 90—
Having had 13 children, 101 grandchildren, 247 Grate-grandchildren,
And 49 Grate-Grate-Grandchildren, total 410.
Three hundred and Thirty Six survived her.
MARY BUEL, LITCHFILED, CONNECTICUT

~

Mary Randolph Keith Marshall
Wife of Thomas Marshall, by whom she had
Fifteen children
Was born in 1737 and died in 1807
She was good but not brilliant
Useful but not great
MARY RANDOLPH KEITH MARSHALL,
MOTHER OF JOHN MARSHALL, WASHINGTON, KY

☾

Here lies Du Vall: Reader, if male thou art,
Look to thy purse, if female, to thy heart.
Much havoc has he made of both, for all
Men he made stand, and woman he made fall.
CLAUDE DU VALL, ST. PAUL'S CHURCHYARD,
COVENT GARDEN, LONDON, ENGLAND

❧

Pray you all
For the vicar's daughter
Millicent Ann
Who died as pure
as they day began.

Added at a later date:

Not afore, in this village, she had every man.
ANONYMOUS

Here lies the body of Mary Jones
For her death held no terrors
Born a virgin, died a virgin
No hits, no runs, no errors
UNVERIFIABLE

❧

To the four husbands
Of Miss Ivy Sanders
1790, 1794, 1808, 18??
Here lies my husbands one, two, three
Dumb as men could ever be;
As for my fourth, well, praise be God
He bides for a little above the sod;
Alex, Ben, Sandy were the first three's names
And to make things tidy, I'll add his—James.
SHUTESBURY, MASSACHUSETTS

~

Although not the mother of the children herself,
she was one busy woman:

In memory of Phoebe Crewe
Who died May 28, 1817, aged 77 years.
Who during forty years practice
As a midwife in this city, brought
Into the world 9,730 children.
PHOEBE CREWE, NORWICH, ENGLAND

SEVEN

HOW'D IT HAPPEN?

It's not modern custom to include cause of death in epitaphs and obituaries but sometimes how it happened gets carved in stone. I doubt that any of us would like to be remembered for circumstances such as these.

Sacred to the memory of
Nathaniel Godbold, Esq.
Inventor & Proprietor of
That excellent medicine
THE VEGETABLE BALSAM
Reknowned for the cure of Consumption
And Asthma
Died Dec. 17, 1799
Died of fevers and asthma
Godalming, England—

☾

Here lies JOHN ROSS
Kicked by a hoss
John Ross, Kendel Parish Church,
Westmoreland, England

✍

Let this small monument record the name
Of CADMAN, and to future times proclaim
How by an attempt to fly from this high spire,
Across the Sabrine stream, he did acquire,
His fatal end. 'Twas not for want of skill,
Or courage to perform the task, he fell;
No, no; a faulty cord being drawn too tight,
Hurried his soul on high to take her flight,
Which bid the body here good-night.
Feb. 2nd, 1739, aged 28.
Anonymous, St. Mary's Church,
Shrewsbury, England

Two great physicians first
My loving husband tried,
To cure my pain—
In vain,
At last he got a third
And then I died.
Molly Dickie, Cheltenham Graveyard,
Gloucester, England

❧

I was a Quack, and there are men who say
That in my time I physicked them away,
And that at length I by myself was slain
By my own doing te'en to relieve my pain
The truth is, being troubled with a cough,
I, like a fool, consulted Dr. Gough,
Who physicked to death at his own will,
Because he's licensed by the state to kill.
Had I but wisely taken my own physisck
I never should have died of cold and 'tisick.
So be warned, and when you catch a cold
Go to my son, by whom medicine's sold.
Anonymous, Carlisle Cemetery, Cumberland, England

∿

O fatal gun, why was it he
That you should kill so dead?
Why didn't you go just a little higher
And fire above his head?
Anonymous, supposedly in Vermont

☾

Poor Martha Snell! Hers gone away,
Her would if her could, but her couldn't stay;
Her'd two sore legs and a baddish cough
But her legs it was that carried her off.
Martha Snell, Chulmleigh Parish Church, Devon, England

Here lies the body of William Beck
He was thrown at a hunt and broke his neck.
WILLIAM BECK, IPSWICH CEMETERY,
SUFFOLK, ENGLAND

❧

Here I lies and my two daughters
Killed by drinking Cheltenham waters;
If we had struck to Epsom salts,
We shouldn't be lying in these vaults.
DONALD ROBERTSON, ST. GILES CHURCH,
CHELTENHAM, GLOUCESTERSHIRE, ENGLAND

❧

Fear God, keep the commandments, and
Don't attempt to climb a tree,
For that caused the death of me.
ANONYMOUS, IN KENT, ENGLAND

❧

Sudden and unexpected was the end
Of our esteemed and beloved friend
He gave to all his friends a sudden shock
By one day falling into Sunderland Dock.
ANONYMOUS, WHITBY CHURCHYARD,
YORKSHIRE, ENGLAND

☾

Here lies Johnny Cole,
Who died, on my soul,
After eating a plentiful dinner,
While showing his crust
He was turned into dust,
With his crimes undigested, poor sinner
JOHNNY COLE, TIPTREE PARISH CHURCH,
ESSEX, ENGLAND

Here lies the body of Jonathan Stout.
He fell in the water and never got out,
And still is supposed to be floating about.
ANONYMOUS, SOMEWHERE
IN CONNECTICUT

❧

This grave holds Caspar Schink, who came to dine,
And taste the noblest vintage of the Rhine;
Three nights he sat, and thirty bottles drank,
Then lifeless by the board of Bacchus sank:
One only comfort have we in the case—
The trump will raise him in the proper place.
ANONYMOUS,
HOCKHEIM CHURCHYARD,
SOMEWHERE IN GERMANY

❧

She was not smart, she was not fair,
But hearts with grief for her are swellin';
All empty stands her little chair,
She died of eatin' water melon.
ANONYMOUS,
NEW JERSEY

Stay away from those melons:

This deceased you ne'er heard tell on
I died of eating too much mellon,
Be careful then, all you that feed, I
Suffered because I was too greedy.
ANONYMOUS,
CHIGWELL CEMETERY,
ESSEX, ENGLAND

Here lies Ned Rand, who on a sudden
Left off roast beef for hasty pudding;
Forsook old stingo, mild and stale
And every drink for Adam's ale;
Till flesh and blood reduced to batter,
Consisting of mere flour and water
Which wanting salt to keep out must
And heat to bake it to a crust
Mouldered and crumbled into dust
Anonymous, Bedlington Church,
Northumberland, England

~

Here lies interred
The body of
Mary Haselton
A young maiden of this town
Born of Roman Catholic parents
And virtuously brought up
Who being in
The act of prayer
Repeating her vespers
Was instantaneously
Killed by a flash of lightning
August 16, 1785
Mary Haselton,
St. Edmond's Churchyard, England

☾

Here lies the body of Emily White
She signaled left, and turned right
Emily White, Location Unknown,
probably spurious

Here lies JOHN ADAMS, who received a thump,
Right on the forehead, from the parish pump,
Which gave him quietus in the end,
For many doctors did his case attend.
JOHN ADAMS, LOCATION UNKNOWN

❧

As you are in health and spirits gay,
I was, too, the other day;
I thought myself of life as safe
As those that read my epitaph.
ANONYMOUS, BYFIELD CHURCH,
NORTHAMPTONSHIRE, ENGLAND

❧

Shoot-Em-Up Jake
Run for Sheriff 1872
Run from Sheriff 1876
Buried 1876
ANONYMOUS, DODGE CITY, KANSAS

❧

Eliza, sorrowing widow, rears this marble slab
To her dear JOHN, who died of eating crab.
ANONYMOUS, PENNSYLVANIA, ALSO REPORTED IN CONSETT
CEMETERY, DURHAM, ENGLAND

☾

Here lie the bones
Of Donald Jones
The wale o'men
For eating scones.
Eating scones
And drinking ale
Till his last moans
He took his fill.
ANONYMOUS, SKYE CEMETERY, SCOTLAND

Jack
Wagner
Killed
Ed Masterson
April 9, 1878
Killed by
Bat Masterson
April 9, 1878
He argued with
The wrong man's
Brother.
JACK WAGNER
DODGE CITY, KANSAS

❧

Mule Skinner Pete
He made the mistake
Of not keeping
His eye on the mule.
ANONYMOUS,
DODGE CITY, KANSAS

❧

Hanged by mistake.
GEORGE JOHNSON, BOOT HILL,
TOMBSTONE, ARIZONA

～

Here lies Butch
We planted him raw
He was quick on the trigger
But slow on the draw
ANONYMOUS

The wedding day
Decided was,
The wedding wine provided
But ere the day did
Come along
He drunk it up and
Died did
Ah Sidney! Ah Sidney
SIDNEY SNYDER, PROVIDENCE,
RHODE ISLAND, 1823.

*Another, curiously similar, yet not as amusing epitaph reportedly
can be found in Bideford Churchyard in Devon, England:*

The wedding day appointed was,
And wedding clothes provided;
But ere the day did come, alas!
He sickened and he died did.

☾

Here lies a man whose
Crown was won
By blowing in an empty gun
ANONYMOUS

❧

In memory of David Dean
July 2, 1783 in ye 27th year of his age
Nine feet high upon a stage
Active in health in bloom of age
But suddenly the stage gave way
He falls, he dies, here ends his days.
DAVID DEAN, EAST TAUTON,
MASSACHUSETTS

The young gentleman referred to here
Killed himself by drinking October beer.
Here lie I must
Wrapp'd up in dust
Confined to be sober.
Clerk take care
Lest you come here,
For faith here's no October.
ANONYMOUS, MIDDLETON-IN-TEESDALE,
DURHAM, ENGLAND

❧

In Memory of Mr.
Neh. Hobart, who died
Ja. 6, 1789 in the 72yr
Of his age
Whose death was caused by
Falling backwards on a
Stick as he was loading wood
Nobody present but his grandson
Who lived with him
A kind husband, a tender parent
A trusty friend, respectable in his day
His death remarkable
NEHEMIAH HOBART,
FOXBORO, MASSACHUSETTS

〜

In Memory of Captain Underwood
Who was drowned
Here lies free from blood and slaughter
Once Underwood—now underwater.
CAPTAIN UNDERWOOD, SUSSEX, ENGLAND

Died of a fever, occasioned
By drinking cold water
On a hot day
STEPHEN RICHARDSON,
WOBURN, MASSACHUSETTS

Seems as if this wive's tale was firmly believed:

Here sleeps in peace a Hampshire grenadier
Who caught his death by drinking cold small beer.
Soldiers be wise from this untimely fall,
And when you're hot drink strong or none at all.
ANONYMOUS, CATHEDRAL YARD,
WINCESTER, ENGLAND

☾

My grandfather lies buried here,
My cousin Jane, and two uncles dear;
My father perish'd with the inflammation of the thighs,
And my sister dropt down dead in the Minories.
But the reason I'm here interr'd according to my thinking,
Is owing to my good living and hard drinking;
If, therefore, good Christians, you wish to live long,
Don't drink too much wine, brandy, gin or anything strong.
ANONYMOUS,
THETFORD CHURCHYARD,
SUFFOLK, ENGLAND

Little
Joe Blackburn
Killed 1871
From where he
Stood he
Saw the moon
Above the caliboose
Looking down
In brilliant
Unconcern
As all Hell was
Breaking loose
Joe Blackburn,
somewhere in Kansas

❧

Tom Henry
185?–1872
Shot by the Sheriff
In a Saloon fight
He was just
A wild kid
Tom Henry,
also somewhere in Kansas

❧

Dead Eye
Steve O'Hara
Killed 1875
Red-Eye ruined
His dead-eye
And he was killed
In a fair fight
Steve O'Hara,
again, Kansas

In memory of
Richard Fothergill
Who met vierlent death
Near this spot
18 hundred and 40 too
he was shot by a pistil
it was not one of the
new kind, but an old
fashioned brass barrill
of such is the kingdom of heaven
RICHARD FOTHERGILL, NEAR SPARTA DIGGINGS, CALIFORNIA.
ALSO REPORTED AS THE GRAVE OF JOHN SMITH, IN THE SAME
LOCATION. HE IS IDENTIFIED AS A GOLD DIGGER.

~

Here lies John Coil
A son of toil
Who died on Arizona soil
He was a man of considerable vim
But this here air was too hot for him
JOHN COIL,
LOCATION UNKNOWN

☾

Kiss me and I will go to sleep
Alice
First and Last
Wife of
Thos. Phillip
Talked to death by friends
ANONYMOUS, PRITCHITT CEMETERY,
BOULDER, ILLINOIS

Erected in memory of
Capt. Thomas Stetson
Who was killed by the fall
Of a tree November 28, 1820
Aet. 68
Nearly 30 years he was the master
Of a vessel and left that
Employment at the age
of 48 for the less hazardous
one of cultivating a farm
Man is never secure
From the arrest of death
Thomas Stetson, Carter Cemetery,
Harvard, Massachusetts

❧

John Blair
Died of smallpox
Cowboy throwed a rope
Over feet and dragged him
To his grave
John Blair, Boothill Cemetery,
Tombstone, Arizona

❧

Andrew C. Hand
Born March 12th, 1842
That Cherry Tree of luscious fruit
Beguiled him too high a branch did break
And down he fell and broke his neck
And died July 13th, 1862
Andrew C. Hand,
Mt. Pleasant Cemetery,
Newark, New Jersey

Beneath these stones repose the bones
Of Theodosius Grimm
He took his bier from year to
Year
And then his bier took him.
THEODOSIUS GRIMM, DURHAM CHURCHYARD, ENGLAND

Here lies Walter Gunn,
Sometimes landlord of the Tun;
Sic transit Gloria mundi
He drank hard upon a Friday
That being a high day,
Then too to his bed
And died upon Sunday
WALTER GUNN, BLYTH CEMETERY,
NORTHUMBERLAND, ENGLAND

Here lies entombed old Roger Norton
Whose sudden death was oddly brought on
Trying one day his corn to mow off
The razor slipped and cut his toe off
The toe, or rather what it grew to
An inflammation quickly flew to
The part affected took to mortifying
And poor old Roger took to dying.
ROGER NORTON, ACTON CHURCHYARD, CORNWALL, ENGLAND.
IT IS ALSO SAID TO BE THE GRAVE OF RICHARD LAWTON,
MORETON-IN-THE-MARSH, GLOUSTERSHIRE, ENGLAND

Constance Bevon, wife of John
Lies beneath this marble stone
Fat and busom, round and stout
'twas apoplexy bowled her out
CONSTANCE BEVON, LOCATION UNKNOWN

JOHN ADAMS lies here, of the parish of Southwell,
A carrier who carried his can to his mouth well;
He carried so much and he carried so fast,
He could carry no more—so was carried at last!
For the liquor he drunk, being too much for one
He could not carry-off—so he's now carrion.
JOHN ADAMS, SOUTHWELL CEMETERY,
DORSET, ENGLAND

Here lies cut down like and unripe fruit
The wife of Deacon Amos Shute
She died from drinking too much coffee
Anny Domini—eighteen-foghty
SARAH SHUTE, CANAAN, CONNECTICUT,
ALSO REPORTED IN BEDRULE PARISH CHURCH,
ROXBURGH, SCOTLAND

Her husband Amos' tomb reads:

He heard the angels calling him
For the Celestial Shore
He flapped his wings and away he went
To make one angel more.

He joined Sarah in 1842.

JOHN ROSE
Died Jan. 27, 1810
Aged 10 years
Dear friends and companions all
Pray warning take by me
Don't venture on the ice too far
As 'twas the death of me
JOHN ROSE, LOCATION UNKNOWN

In memory of Mr. Nath. Parks
Aet. 19 who on the 21st March 1797
Being out a hunting and concel'd
In a ditch was casually shot
By Mr. Luther Frink
Nathan Parks, Elmwood Cemetery,
Holyoke, Massachusetts

☾

Here in this urn
From Malaber
The ashes lie
of Jonathan Barr
He sought a higher life
Afar
And traveled home
In a jar
Jonathan Barr, Nantucket, Rhode Island

❧

Reader, Death took me without any warning
I was well at night and died in the morning
Anonymous, Frome Churchyard, England

❧

Here I lie
No wonder I'm dead
For a broad wheeled wagon
Went over my head
Grim death took me
With out a warning
I was well and night
And dead in the morning.
15 March 1797
John Wight, Sevenoaks Churchyard,
Kent, England

Here I lie
And no wonder I'm dead
I fell from a tree
Roll'd over dead
MARVIN WESTERBROOK,
AROOSTOOK COUNTY, MAINE, 1824

1891
shot in the back
by a dirty rat
CHARLES THOMPSON, NAINAIMO,
BRITISH COLUMBIA, CANADA

Here under the dung of cows and sheep
Lies an old high climber fast asleep
His trees all topped and his lines all hung
They say the old rascal died full of rum
PAUL LENNIS SWANK, CANYONVILLE CEMETERY,
CANYONVILLE, OREGON

Here lies Rastus Sominy
Died a-eatin hominy
In 1859 anno domini
RASTUS SOMINY, SAVANNAH, GEORGIA

Born 1903–Died 1942
Looked up an elevator shaft to see if the
Car was on the way down. It was
HARRY EDSEL SMITH,
ALBANY, GEORGIA

Who was fatally burned
March 21, 1870
By the explosion of a lamp
Filled with "R.E. Danforth's
Non-explosive burning fluid."
Ellen Shannon, Girard, Pennsylvania

~

Donald Robertson
Born 1st of January, 1765, died 4th June, 1848
Aged 83 years
He was a peaceable and quiet man, and to all appearance
A sincere Christian.
His death was very much regretted,
which was caused by the stupidity of Laurence Tulloch
Of Clotherton, who sold him nitre instead of Epsom
Salts, by which he was killed in the space of
3 hours after taking a dose of it.
Donald Robertson, Crosskirk,
Shetland, Scotland 1785, aged 63 years

☾

Here lies Sir John Plumpudding
Of the Grange
Who hanged himself one morning
For a change
Sir John Plumpudding,
location unknown and a tad bit spurious

This is another one of the spurious tombstones from Tombstone, a clever little play on a name:

Here lies Lester Moore
Four slugs from a forty-four
No Less no More
Lester Moore, Boothill Cemetery,
Tombstone, Arizona, 1880

Here lies the body of Henry Moore
Who got in the way of a 44
Princess Anne County, Virginia

❦

The Lord saw God,
I was lopping off wood,
And fell from the tree:
I met with a check & I broke my neck
And so death lopped off me
John Martin, Ockham,
England 1787

↷

A victim of fast women and slow horses
Milt MacPhail, Teck Township Cemetery,
Kirkland Lake, Ontario, Canada

∽

Here lies the body of
Mary Ann Louder
She burst while drinking
A Seidlitz powder;
Called from this world
To her heavenly rest
She drank it and
She effervesced
Mary Anne Lowder,
Burleigh, New Jersey, 1880

There is a variation of this stone on which the final line apparently reads: she should have waited till it effervesced. Another one puts the date of this woman's death as 1798 in Burlington, Massachusetts and names her Susan, but Siedlitz Powder wasn't on the market till 1824.

Grim Death
To please his liquorish palate
Has taken my Lettice
To put in his salad
LETICIA, ANONYMOUS

☾

On the 29th of November
A confounded piece of timber
Came down, bang slam
And killed I, John Lamb
JOHN LAMB, HUNTINGTON,
ENGLAND 1700

🐿

Here lies the body of Thomas Kemp
Who lived by wool and died by hemp;
There nothing would suffice the glutton
But with the fleece to steal the mutton;
Had he but worked and lived uprighter
He'd ne'er been hung for a sheep-biter.
THOMAS KEMP, BELLINGHAM PARISH CHURCHYARD,
NORTHUMBERLAND, ENGLAND

🐦

Smith of Smoketown
He smoked his cigarette till
From it came
That subtle venom spreading
From its flame
Which poisoned every fibre
Of his frame
And laid him low
Yet whilst he smoked
He languishly sighed
It is but paper round tobacco plied
When like a flicker of a lamp
He died and rests below.
JOHN JONES, UNVERIFIED

Who was carelessly run over
And killed returning from the races
May 21st, 1831 Aged 21 years
O Henecy! You did me kill
And would not pay my dokter's bill
WILLIAM JACKSON, BOTANY CEMETERY,
NEW SOUTH WALES, AUSTRALIA

⁓

Here lies the body of our Anna
Done to death by a banana
It wasn't the fruit that laid her low
But the skin of the thing that made
Her go
ANNA HOPEWELL, ENOSBURG FALLS, VERMONT
ALSO REPORTED IN ITHACA, NEW YORK.

☾

Here lies Matthew Hollingshead
Who died from a cough caught in his head
It brought on fever and Rheumatiz
Which ended me—for here I is.
MATTHEW HOLLINGSHEAD, LOCATION UNKNOWN

❧

To the memory of
Dennis McCabe, fiddler
Who fell out of the St. Patrick Barge, belonging to
Sir James Caldwell, Bart., and Count of Milan, and
Was drowned off this point, August ye 13, 1770
Beware ye fiddler's of ye fiddler's fate
Nor tempt ye deep lest ye repent too late
Ye ever have been deemed to water foes
Then shun ye lake till it with whiskey floes
On firm land only exercise your skill
There ye may play and drink your fill
CASTLE CALDWELL, LOUGH ERNE, IRELAND

Against his will
Here lies George Hill
Who from a cliff
Fell down quite stiff
GEORGE HILL, ST. JOSEPH CHURCH,
KINGSTON-UPON-THAMES, SURREY, ENGLAND

❧

Peaceable and Quiet, a friend to his
Father and mother, and respected
By all who knew him, and went
To the world where horses don't kick . . .
HENRY HARRIS, ROSS PARK CEMETERY,
WILLIAMSPORT, PENNSYLVANIA, 1837

～

Murdered near this town June 15, 1808
His murderers were never discovered.
You villains! If this stone you see
Remember that you murdered me!
You bruised my head and pierced my heart
Also my bowels did suffer part
JOSEPH GLEDOWING,
WORKINGTON, ENGLAND, 1808

☾

Samuel Gardner was blind in one eye
And in a moment of confusion
He stepped out of a receiving
And discharging door in one of the
Warehouses into the ineffable
Glories of the celestial sphere.
SAMUEL GARDINER, LOCATION UNKNOWN

𖤓

Was killed by the cars
ADAM FREY, HARTFORD MEMORIAL CEMETERY, WISCONSIN

Here doth lye the bodie
Of John Flye, who did die
By a stroke from a sky-rocket
Which hit him in the eye-socket
JOHN FLYE, DURNESS CHURCHYARD,
SUTHERLANDSHIRE, ENGLAND, 1680

❧

Here lies the remains of
Marshall Miller
The husband, the parent, the friend
He exercised virtues in the age sufficient
To have distinguished in the best
Kind & tender nature
Industrious by habit
Professing religion
He departed his life
June 10th, 1807 Aged 53
He died in Saratoga, in the state of N. York
His death occasioned by jumping from a window,
In the 5th story of a house
Which was on fire
MARSHALL MILLER,
DUMMERSTON, VERMONT

～

In memory of the clerk's son—
Bless my I, I, I, I, I, I,
Here I lies
In a sad pickle
Killed by an icicle.
ANONYMOUS, BAMPTON,
DEVON, ENGLAND

Here lies interred a man o'micht
They ca'd him Malcome Downie
He lost his life ae market nicht
By fa'in aff his pownie
Aged 37 years.
MALCOME DOWNIE, CULLEN GRAVEYARD,
BANFFSHIRE, ENGLAND

☾

Beneath this stone a lump of clay
Lies Uncle Peter Daniels
Who early in the month of May
Took off his winter flannels
PETER DANIELS, EDINBURGH, SCOTLAND; ALSO REPORTED IN
CHATHAM CEMETERY, KENT, ENGLAND

❧

She failed her breathalyzer test
Now she lays with the best
JEANINE CUSTIS, ROSE HILL CEMETERY,
NEWBURY, INDIANA

❧

His death was produced
By being spured in the head
By a rooster
DAVID CORBIN, OLD SCHOOL BAPTIST CHURCHYARD,
ROXBURY, NEW YORK

～

'Twas as she tript from cask to cask
In a bung-hole quickly fell
Suffocation was her task
She had no time to say farewell
ANN COLLINS, KING STANLEY CHURCHYARD, GLOUCESTERSHIRE,
ENGLAND, DIED SEPT. 11, 1804, AGED 49

Here lies the body of
Jonathan Blake
Stepped on the gas pedal
Instead of the brake
Jonathan Blake,
Uniontown, Pennsylvania

☾

To all my friends
I bid adieu
A more sudden death
You never knew:
As I was leading
The mare to drink
She kicked and killed me
Quicker'n a wink
Anonymous, Melton Mowbray Parish Church,
Oxford, England

❧

The manner of her death was thus
She was druv over by a bus
Anonymous

❧

He rests in pieces
Anonymous

❧

A bird, a man, a loaded gun
No bird, dead man
Thy will be done
Anonymous

Here lies a man who was killed
By lightning;
He died when his prospects seemed to
Be brightening.
He might have cut a flash in this
World of trouble,
But the flash cut him, and he lies
In the stubble.
Anonymous, Great Torrington Church, Devon, England

☾

Blown upward
Out of sight
He sought the leak
By candlelight
Anonymous, Collingbourne Ducis Cemetery,
Wiltshire, England

❧

He got a fishbone
In his throat
Which made him sing
An angel's note
Anonymous, reported in Schenectady, New York

❧

He called
Bill Smith
A Liar
Anonymous, Cripple Creek, Colorado

〜

There good old woman of Ryde
ate some apples and died
The apples fermented inside the lamented
Made cider inside her inside
Anonymous, Ryde Churchyard, Isle of Wight

EIGHT

SHARP TONGUES

*Some of these people died angry,
or at least slightly miffed, and used
the grave-cutter's chisel to share
their grievances with the world.
Others just couldn't be bothered.*

Randsom Beardsley
Died Jan. 24, 1850
Aged 56 yr 7 mo 21 days
A vol. in the war of 1812
No pension
RANSOM BEARDSLEY, MOTTVILLE, MICHIGAN

☾

Eleazer Albee
Born Rockingham, Vermont
Died Stanstead
Aug. 28, 1864
He went into voluntary Banishment from his
Beloved Native Country, during the
Reigning Terror in the Third year of the
Misrule of Abraham the First
AND DIED SHORTLY THEREAFTER:
ELEAZER ALBEE, STANSTEAD, QUEBEC, CANADA

❧

Let medical science loom up
High as it will
The order of Quacks
Will attend to it still
JOHN AND RALPH AKERS,
OASIS CEMETERY, WEST BRANCH, IOWA

❧

Killed by an unskilled Dr.
FRANCES CERNY, ST. MARY'S CEMETERY, WINONA, MINNESOTA, 1902

∼

What! Kill a partridge in the
month of May, Not quite
sportsman like
Eh, Death, Eh?
THOMAS PARTRIDGE, REPORTEDLY IN LUDLOW, SHROPSHIRE, ENGLAND

She always said her feet were killing
Her but nobody believed her.
MARGARET DANIELS, HOLLYWOOD CEMETERY,
RICHMOND, VIRGINIA

☾

Reader, pass on, nor waste your
Precious time
On bad biography and murdered rhyme
What I was before's well known to
My neighbors
What I am now is no concern of yours.
WILLIAM ASH, DEVON, ENGLAND 1797

🐌

Another very similar:
Reader pass on an ne'er waste your time
On bad biography and bitter rhyme
For what I am this cumb'rous clay insures
And what I was, is no affair of yours
MARY LEFAVOUR, TOPSFIELD, MASSACHUSETTS 1797 AGED 74. ALSO
REPORTED OVER THE TOMB OF MARY BURGESS, AT ST. MARGARET'S
CHURCHYARD IN IPSWICH, ENGLAND, DEC. 25, 1825

↶

I was somebody
Who is no business of yours
ANONYMOUS, STOWE, VERMONT

⌁

SSGT US Air Force
Feb 28 1950–Aug 3 1998
THIS ATM IS CLOSED
DANIEL STEVEN BURLEY,
LOS ANGELES, CALIFORNIA

101st Infantry Division
Yankee Division—Massachusetts
Pioneer in Television 1951–1987
September 15, 1922–December 7, 1988
I'm fine, thank you
SGT VINCE E. BUSHEY, LOS ANGELES, CALIFORNIA

☾

Now Ain't
That too bad
CHARLES DUPLESSIS, ROSEHILL CEMETERY,
CHICAGO, ILLINOIS, 1907

✿

Life is a jest and all things show it
I thought so once, and now I know it
JOHN GAY, WESTMINSTER ABBEY,
LONDON, ENGLAND

❧

Go away—I'm Asleep.
JOAN HACKETT, HOLLYWOOD MEMORIAL PARK,
LOS ANGELES, CALIFORNIA

∽

Hey, reader, turn your weeping eyes,
My fate a useful moral teaches;
The hole in which my body lies
Would not contain half my speeches.
LORD BROUGHAM, GRASMERE CHURCH,
WESTMORELAND, ENGLAND

In this house
Which I have borrowed from
My brethren, the worms,
Lie I
Samuel, by divine permission,
Bishop of this Island
Stop, reader:
Behold and smile at
The palace of a bishop!
Who died May 30, in the year 1653
Dr. Samuel Rutter, Bishop of Sodor and Man,
St. Germain's, Isle of Man

☾

Here lies
Hermine Kuntz
To virtue quite unkown
Jesus Rejoice!
At last
She sleeps alone.

Spurious and completely unverifiable, and the name, well it just HAS to be made up.

🐚

Anything for a change.
Anonymous, New Gray Cemetery,
Knoxville, Kentucky

🕊

I don't want to talk about it now.
Bonnie Anderson, Forest Lawn Cemetery,
Hollywood Hills, Los Angeles, California

Here lies Ezekiel Aikle
Age 102
The good
Die young
EZEKIEL AIKLE, EAST DALHOUSIE CEMETERY,
NOVA SCOTIA

~

NORTON I
Emperor of the United States
And Protector of Mexico
JOSHUA NORTON, THE MASONIC CEMETERY, COLMA, CALIFORNIA,
1880

Old Norton was a San Francisco eccentric who declared himself Emperor. Humored by the townspeople, they even accepted the bank notes he issued for himself.

☾

Old & Still
NICHOLAS EVE, PARISH BURIAL GROUND,
KITTERY POINT, MAINE, 1880

❧

Quid Eram, Nescitis
Quid sum, Sescitis:
Ubi Abbi, Nescitis:
Valete!
(What I was, you know not
what I am, you know not:
Whither I am gone, you know not:
Go about your business!).
MICAH HALL, CARLETON,
ENGLAND, 1804

Stranger pause, my tale attend
And learn the cause of Hannah's end
Across the world the wind did blow
she ketched a cold that laid her low
We shed a lot of tears tis true
But life is short—aged 82.
ANONYMOUS

❧

Here lyeth ye body of
Sarah Bloomfield
Aged 74
Cut off in blooming youth; we can but pity.
SARAH BLOOMFIELD, ST. NICHOLAS,
YARMOUTH, ENGLAND, 1675

～

Asenth Soule
Widow of
Simeon Soule
Died Feb. 25, 1865
Aged
87 years, 11 mo.
& 19 days.
The chisel can't help her any.
ASENTH SOULE,
MAYFLOWER CEMETERY,
DUXBURY, MASSACHUSETTS, 1865

Al Shean
Beloved Father
Born May 12, 1868
I could have lived longer
But now it's too late
Absolutely, Mr. Gallagher—Positively Mr. Shean
August 12, 1949
AL SHEAN, MOUNT PLEASANT CEMETERY,
PLEASANTVILLE, NEW YORK

The penultimate line is the tag line of his famous Ziegfield Follies act with Ed Gallagher.

☾

He posesed
Many good Qualitys
But as he was a man
He had the frailities
Common to mans nature.
ADAM ALLYN, TRINITY CHURCHYARD,
NEW YORK, 1768

NINE

END
OF
STORY

The deathbed is a place for statements that
are occasionally existential, sometimes dead-
pan, often profound, and always interesting.
Most of the people quoted in this chapter faced
death with humor and aplomb, except those,
who, taken utterly off guard, went out with
the age-old adage, "Aw, crap!"

In a 1925 article for *Vanity Fair*, W.C. Fields suggested his own epitaph: "On the whole, I would rather be living in Philadelphia." Forty one years later, his actual last words were, "God damn the whole friggin' world and everyone in it." With a final thought to his mistress, "Except you, Carlotta!"

((

Once a baseball fan, always a baseball fan: Morris Berg, a famous catcher for the Boston Red Sox and former spy's final words were, "How'd the Mets do today?"

ℳ

Elizabeth (Betsy) Patterson-Bonaparte, wife of the brother of Napoleon and daughter of a rich Baltimore, Maryland merchant, reportedly repeated the old cliché, "Nothing is so certain as death, except taxes," upon her deathbed.

✤

Wild West legend William F. Cody, known to all as Buffalo Bill, was incredulous, but in good spirits, when the doctors told him how long he had to live. He replied, "Thirty-six hours? That's all? Well, let's forget about it and play high five."

〜

Scottish scientist James Croll saw a round of drinks going about in his Perth, Scotland sick room. He was known as a teetotaler, but he figured it couldn't hurt him and said, "I'll take a wee drop o'that. I don't think there's much fear of me learning to drink now."

((

Massachusetts governor James Michael Curley, apparently appalled at the state of the floors in the hospital he had been taken to, was a politician to the end. From his gurney he stated, "I wish to announce the first plank in my campaign for reelection—we're going to have the floors in this god-damned hospital smoothed."

Conductor Pablo Casals' final ride, in an ambulance, didn't suit his fancy: "The driver's a maniac. He'll kill us all!"

❧

Playwright Eugene O'Neill, the son of a well-known actor, was born in a hotel room on Broadway. For a writer who often depicted characters at the hopeless whim of destiny, his final words may be too coincidental to be funny. On his deathbed in a hotel room in Boston, O'Neill declared "I knew it! I knew it! Born in a goddamn hotel room, and dying in a hotel room!"

❧

Hollywood screenwriter and producer, Henry Mankiewicz, gave detailed instructions on his deathbed. "Assuming the ceremony will be held indoors, hats will not be worn, except that Dore Schary will wear his hat. You are to go up to Dore Schary and tap him on the shoulder and say, 'Dore, I have a message for you from the deceased: Take off your hat, you're in the house.'"

❧

In and out of consciousness, radical nineteenth-century English statesman Henry Labouchere, was awakened when an oil lamp near his deathbed was knocked over and caught fire. His comment upon waking was, "Flames? Not yet, I think."

☽

As a French Society of Jesus member and teacher of grammar, Dominique Bourhous couldn't get the grammarian out of his system. "I am about to—or I am going to die, either expression is correct."

❧

For a minister and editor who was considered one of the greatest orators of his day, Henry Ward Beecher had surprisingly little to say to his doctor on his deathbed. When asked if he could raise his arm, he replied, "I can raise it high enough to hit you."

Joan Crawford was immortalized as a woman with an angry streak in the 1981 movie, *Mommie Dearest*. She built on her fearsome reputation with her last words. Upon hearing someone praying in her room, she roared, "Damn it . . . don't you dare ask God to help me." (To further her reputation as a bitch, her will stipulated "it [was her] intention to make no provision herein for [her] son Christopher or [her] daughter Christina for reasons which are well known to them.")

❧

"Too many cigars this evening, I guess," were the last words of famed newspaperman, E.W. Scripps.

〜

Nobel Prize winning playwright (he took the prize, but didn't accept the money) George Bernard Shaw philosophized on death that, "Well, it will be a new experience anyway."

☾

It's not certain whether Henry John Temple, Lord Palmerston, British Prime Minister in the 1850s and perpetual irritant to Queen Victoria, was being stubborn or profound (probably stubborn) when he said to his doctor, "Die, my dear doctor? That's the last thing I shall do."

❦

Richard Monckton Milnes, Baron of Houghton, an author and contemporary of John Keats, reminded us of that the cycle of life has to end somewhere with his final words, "my exit is the result of too many entrees."

❧

Henry Fox, 1st Baron of Holland and 18th-century British politician, was cordial with his political rival George Selwyn. When Fox heard that Selwyn had called on him, he stated, "If Mr. Selwyn calls again, show him up; if I am alive I shall be delighted to see him; and if I am dead, he would like to see me."

Robert Erskine Childers was a player during "the Troubles" in Ireland, the beginning of the fight for independent statehood from England. He sided with Eamon DeValera, soon to be the first president of the Republic of Ireland, against the Anglo-Irish treaty brokered by Michael Collins in 1921. The treaty called for a nominal independence of the southern counties, but left out Ulster, and included an oath of allegiance to England. Agreeing that he would settle for nothing less than the total free Irish Republic DeValera and the IRA were fighting for, Childers was sentenced to death for treason. His final words to his firing squad were, "Take a step forward, lads. It will be easier that way."

~

Oil baron J. Paul Getty, although he was the richest man in the world at the time of his death, could be at times a bit surly. His reported last words were an order, "I want my lunch!"

☾

Half of the comedic brilliance that was the team of Laurel and Hardy ("Who's on first?"), Arthur Stanley Jefferson (a.k.a. Laurel) said upon his deathbed that he, "would rather be skiing." When asked if he skied he said, "No, but I'd rather be doing that than doing this."

☙

Orson Welles, probably one of the greatest directors Hollywood will ever see, was understandably proud of his crowning achievement, *Citizen Kane*. Aware of the habits of entertainment mogul Ted Turner, the man who dared to colorize the old black and white classics, Welles said on his deathbed, "Don't let Ted Turner deface my movie with his crayons."

❧

American writer and cartoonist James G. Thurber, whose wonderful creations include the character Walter Mitty and a little book of comic genius written with fellow *New Yorker* writer E.B. White, *Is Sex Necessary?*, was short with his last words. He simply said, "God Bless . . . God Damn!"

Sir Walter Raleigh, an Elizabethan poet and courtier, having previously avoided a death sentence for intrigues against the English crown, came under the derision of the ambassador of Spain, who demanded he be punished for being associated with the capture of a Spanish town. About to be executed for the original sentence of treason, he said of the blade that would sever his neck, "'Tis a sharp remedy, but a sure one for all ills." (Additionally macabre, his wife is reported to have had his head embalmed. She held onto it for the rest of her days and was buried with it.)

Bernard de Fontenelle was a French scholar in the 18th century. "I feel nothing, apart from a certain difficulty in continuing to exist," he said. He was over one hundred years old.

Although not his actual last words, Benjamin Disraeli, a nineteenth-century Prime Minister of Britain, and seeming lapdog to Queen Victoria, was told while awaiting his death that her majesty was there to see him. When asked whether she should be shown up, he replied, "No. Tis better not. She will only ask me to take a message to Alfred" (the Queen's consort).

King Charles II, king of England in the 17th century, felt the need to apologize for how long it was taking his to meet his maker, "I have taken an unconsciousable time dying, but I hope you will excuse it."

German author, Heinrich Heine, was talking to his priest when he said, "Of course God will forgive me. That's his job."

Legend has it that George V, king of England, uttered "Bugger Bognor!" upon his deathbed. Bognor Regis was a resort that the king decided he was not well enough to visit.

Francois Rabelais was a sixteenth-century French writer of satire. His final utterance was, "I owe much, I have nothing, the rest I left to the poor."

((

William Sidney Porter (O' Henry), commentator on the excruciating irony that can be found in life, said "Turn up the lights, I don't want to go home in the dark."

❧

The last words of Kathleen Ferrier, the famous opera singer, belied her profession, "Now, I will have eine kleine Pause."

❧

One would expect a hilarious and sarcastic statement from Oscar Wilde, the renowned Irish author and humorist, but we don't know what they were. We do know he was sickly and dying, a relatively broken man. He reportedly said during his last days two things, one in relation to the room's decor, "Either that wallpaper goes, or I do," and another to a glass of champagne, "It seems I am dying beyond my means."

~

Leo Tolstoy, author of the daunting novel *War and Peace*, is reported to have said, "Even in the valley of the shadow of death, two and two do not make six." Another source has him saying, "The truth . . . I care a great deal . . . how they," which isn't quite as amusing.

((

Poet Dylan Thomas was in a coma, never to awake, but before he slipped into oblivion his dying boast was, "I've had eighteen straight whiskies. I think that's a record."

❧

Lytton Strachey, a British author of biographies, was not impressed when the grim reaper came to call: "If this is dying, then I don't think much of it."

General John Sedgwick, of the Army of the Potomac, reportedly said, moments before a sniper's bullet hit him during the battle of Spotsylvania, "They couldn't hit an elephant at this distance!"

❧

Another soldier, one of Theodore Roosevelt's Rough Riders, too sure of his own imperviousness, said, "Sergeant, there's not a Spanish bullet made that will kill me!"

～

Benjamin Cardoza was a judge till the last, "They tell me I am going to get well, but I file a dissenting opinion."

☾

Brendan Behan was a playwright who exuded his Irish wit until his dying day. To his nurse, a nun, he allegedly said, "Ahh, bless you sister, may all your sons be bishops." He also reportedly said to his wife, "You made one mistake, you married me."

❧

Voltaire, the philosopher/author of *Candide*, famed of France, when asked by his priest whether he had renounced Satan, allegedly said, "Now, now, my good man, this is no time to be making enemies." It is also reported, however, that he said to the priest, whose presence was not welcome, "In God's name, let me die in peace," and turning his head to the side of the bed where there was a lamp, finished his life with the words, "the flames already?"

❧

Another philosopher-poet, America's Henry David Thoreau, was asked the opposite—if he had made peace with God, to which he replied, "I did not know that we had quarreled." (This is reported on his deathbed as one of his last statements. His very last words, however, reflected the years he spent communing with nature. The non sequitur, "Moose! Indian!" was the last utterance to pass his lips.)

Gertrude Stein, briefly awake, looked at her long time-lover Alice B. Toklas, and asked, "What is the answer?" She received no answer. Her last words were, "In that case, what is the question?"

Famed showman of "The Greatest Show on Earth," ever the business man, Phineas T. Barnum, asked his companion, "How were the circus receipts at Madison Square Garden?"

Francis Crowley, bank robber and momma's boy, said, just before his execution, "You sons of bitches. Give my love to mother."

Executed by hanging, William Palmer walked to the gallows and asked his executioner, "Are you sure this is safe?"

Thomas de Mahay, Marquis de Favras, executed during the French Revolution, had enough wits about him on his way to the guillotine to point out that the court had erred on his official death sentence. He pointed out, "I see that you have made three spelling mistakes."

"Shoot straight you bastards and don't make a mess of it," were the last words of condemned Australian convict Harry Morant.

A member of the mob, Arnold Rothstein, the man who supposedly fixed the famed game in 1919 that destroyed the Chicago White Sox, was shot and dying. He was asked by law-enforcement, "Who shot you?" Never wanting the stigma of being a stool pigeon to be put upon him said, "Me Mudder did it."

With less of his wits about him, another gangster, Dutch Schultz, a.k.a. Arthur Fleigenheimer, shot by Lucky Luciano's gang, rambled incoherently till his demise, saying such unconnected phrases as, "Turn your back to me, please. Henry, I am so sick now. The police are getting many complaints. Look out I want that G-note. Look out for Jimmy Valentine, for he's a friend of mine. Come on, come on, Jim. Okay, okay, I am all through. I can't do another thing. Look out mamma. Look out for her, police, mamma. Helen please take me out. I will settle the incident. Come on, open the soap duckets, the chimney sweeps. Talk to the sword. Shut up, you got a big mouth. Don't let Satan draw you too fast. Please help me get up. Henry! Max! Come over here. French Canadian Bean Soup!"

The infamous union boss, Jimmy Hoffa, whose whereabouts are still unknown (it's been 30 years), boasted in an interview with *Playboy*, that he "don't need no bodyguards." His actual last words were, "Has Tony Giacalone called?"

Servants crying for their king prompted this reaction from "the sun king," Louis XIV, king of France, "Why are you weeping? Did you imagine I was immortal?"

Alexander Pope, eighteenth-century author of *The Rape of the Lock*, supposedly said, "I am dying, sir, of a hundred good symptoms."

Famed American revolutionary, Ethan Allen, was told, in an attempt to calm him, that the angels were waiting for him. He supposedly replied, "Waiting are they? Waiting are they? Well—let them wait!"

John Holmes (no, not the porn star), the brother of famed Supreme Court Justice Oliver Wendell Holmes, was mostly dead when his nurse said that she would feel his feet, to see if they were warm. "Nobody ever died with their feet warm," she is reported to have said. His reply, to the astonishment of all present was, "John Rogers did." John Rogers was burned at the stake. His brother, Oliver, was reported to say, in response to all the medical equipment being employed to save his life, "Just a lot of damnfoolery!"

❧

Never ask a dying man who he would rather have at the side of his deathbed as he passes. You might get the reply Henry Arthur Jones, an English playwright, gave his niece and nurse the day he died. "The prettier. Now fight for it."

〜

There are times when a priest's presence is not appreciated. Wilson Minzer, didn't need one. His last words to his priest were, "Why should I talk to you? I was just speaking to your boss." (Prior to that he had said to his doctor "Well, doc, I guess this is the main event.")

☾

Another poor priest got a worse putdown from composer Jean-Phillipe Rameau, who couldn't handle the father's monotonous singing. The musician said to him, "What the devil do you mean singing to me, priest? You are out of tune."

❧

James Scott, the Duke of Monmouth, was executed for rebellion against Charles II, king of England. Following a friend and acquaintance to the chopping block, he was well aware of the unsure hands of some of the executioners. He asked to be spared the pain of mistake by saying, "Prithee, let me feel the axe. I fear it is not sharp enough. Do not hack me like you did my Lord Russell." He supposedly bribed his executioner six guineas to make sure his last request was attended to.

❧

DEAD MEN WALKING: There's a traditional joke at San Quentin, the site of California's infamous death row, that inmates on their way to the gas chamber, would ask for a little bicarbonate of soda from the warden to deal with the gas. Like that joke, these execution quips may well be apocryphal. A man named George Appel's last words were, allegedly, "Well, gentleman, you are about to see a baked apple." And another, a man named James French, was executed in 1966. His last words supposedly were, "How's this for a headline? French Fries." Johnny Frank Garrett, said, "I'd like to thank my family for loving me and taking care of me. The rest of the world can kiss my ass." Gary Gilmore, another death-row victim, said simply, "Let's do it."

~

Death row inmates are given a last meal, whatever they desire. One said inmate made it known to the world that his last request was not fulfilled. His last statement, an admonition of his keepers, relayed, "I did not get my Spaghetti-Os. I got spaghetti. I want the press to know that." Another murderer, named Neville Heath, asked for a whiskey. On second thought he said, "Ahh, you might want to make that a double." And a victim of the French Revolution, Georges-Jacques Danton said on the platform of the guillotine that took his head, "You will show my head to the people; it is worth showing."

☾

James Rogers, another man executed by firing squad for his crimes, was asked if he had any last request, "Why, yes," he said, "A bulletproof vest." Edger Edwards was hanged with the final words, "I've been looking forward to this." Albert Fish, the perpetrator of some of the most heinous crimes of the twentieth century, was put to death with the words, "What a thrill it will be to die in the electric chair, the supreme thrill, the only one I haven't tried yet." (He supposedly set the electrodes upon his head himself). Still another mass murderer, Carl Pazram, hanged in 1930, said, "Hurry it up, you Hoosier bastard! I could hang a dozen men while you're fooling around." Russian revolutionary, Pavel Ivanovich Pestel's first hanging attempt was unsuccessful, and his last words reflected his contempt for his executioners, "Stupid country, where they do not even know how to hang."

❦

Eighteenth-century composer Christopher Gluck had written a piece called *The Last Judgment*, which was being staged as he was dying. He was asked who should sing the role of Jesus, to which he replied, "If you wait a little while, I shall be able to tell you from personal experience."

Winston Churchill, statesman, Prime Minister and leader of the English during World War II, was known for his dry wit. Although his last words were actually, "I am so bored with it all," he reportedly said to his daughter earlier, "I am ready to meet my maker. Whether my maker is prepared for the great ordeal of meeting me is another matter."

❧

The consummate communist, Karl Marx, had written and said enough during his lifetime to satisfy at least himself. His housemaid, on the other hand, wanted one more statement. Karl, was having nothing of it. He admonished her with, "Go on, get out! Last words are for fools who haven't said enough."

❧

William Vanderbilt, son of the tycoon Cornelius Vanderbilt, died poor, bereft, with only $200,000 in his coffer in 1885 [read that again, $200,000 in 1885]. His last statement speaks for itself, "I have had no real gratification or enjoyment of any sort more than my neighbor on the next block who is only worth half a million."

~

Thomas Ketchum, of the old West, a.k.a. Blackjack, knew where his life had taken him, and said to those that would hang him, "I'll be in Hell before you start breakfast, boys! Let her rip."

☾

Henry Plummer was the sheriff in a town in Washington State. The townspeople, tired of his corruption and greed, formed a lynch mob. When they confronted him he asked, "You wouldn't hang your own sheriff, would you?"

❧

Douglas Fairbanks, one of Hollywood's most enduring actors, didn't really know what state he was actually in and informed his visitors that he, "Never felt better."

Wuthering Heights' author Emily Brontë, was known for her stubbornness. She refused medical attention till the nth hour. Her last words were, "If you will send for a doctor, I will see him now."

❧

Heartthrob, swashbuckler, legend, alleged rapist (he was acquitted): Errol Flynn, was pleased with his life. He'd had, "a hell of a lot of fun. And enjoyed every minute of it."

〜

How's this for a send-off? The playwright, George Kelly, must have thought that his niece, Grace Kelly, wife of the Prince of Monaco and famed starlit, was the epitome of fashion and style to the point of taking it out on the rest of his family. Another poor niece, intent on giving him a last, goodbye kiss, was told, "My dear, before you kiss me goodbye, fix your hair. It's a mess."

☾

Sir Lawrence Olivier, quite possibly the greatest Shakespearean actor to grace the stage, was a tad surly and untrue to his public persona, upon his deathbed, yet true to his acting roots. His nurse faltered with the water she brought him and it spilled. His response? "This isn't Hamlet, you know. It's not meant to go in my bloody ear."

❦

Speaking of Shakespeare, Drew Barrymore is one of the current sweethearts of Hollywood and she comes from a long line of actors famous for their stage presence and, well, eccentricities. The apple falls not far from the tree. Her grandfather, John, felt himself more powerful than he should have. His last words mocked the inevitable: "Die? I should say not. No Barrymore would allow such a conventional thing to happen to him."

❧

A saying has come into the English language via Tchaikovsky's immortal ballet, *Swan Lake.* And the one woman who danced it so superbly that she will forever be associated with that moment was Anna Pavlova. She was not unaware of this. In her last moments, knowing that the phrase, swan song, will forever be remember as that last, dying dance, said, "Get my swan costume ready."

French aristocrat and friend of Jean Jacques Rousseau's, the Comtess de Vercellis, would have made a modern woman blush with her last words. Moments after passing gas, without embarrassment, at least to her, she said, "Good. A woman who can fart is not dead."

If you ever fly into New York, you may fly into an airport named after Fiorello LaGuardia, the mayor of the city from 1934–1945. Acerbic, straight-forward, and unapologetic, his last words were to a judge who came to visit him, "I'm glad to meet an honest judge."

Ever so often, someone actually asks the dying person if they have any last words. Conrad Hilton, mogul of the Hilton hotel empire, offered this gem, as only a hotelier could, "Leave the shower curtain on the inside of the tub." The famous voice of Rod Serling greeted countless viewers every week with his intro to the show "The Twilight Zone." Rod, however, wasn't quite ready to enter another dimension when it came his time. "You can't kill this tough Jew," he wrote to a colleague from his hospital bed. He died during an operation soon after.

Is it poetic justice that makes us chuckle at this one? The police officer that escorted the shackled Lee Harvey Oswald who, according to the Warren Report acted alone in his assassination of President John F. Kennedy, reported that Oswald's last words were, "There ain't nobody gonna shoot me." Well, Jack Ruby thought otherwise.

Huey "Kingfish" Long, the not-so-straight dealing governor of Louisiana, was shot in the capitol building in Baton Rouge in 1935 by a man upset that Long's crooked and shadowy dealings had cost his family dearly. "God, don't let me die," Long said, "I have so much to do." As if the poor state of Louisiana hadn't had enough tyranny already. He is also reported-ly said to have uttered, "I wonder why he shot me?"

This really shouldn't be funny. And is probably completely erroneous, because there is no one who can possibly have reported what was said. Even so, had the Darwin Awards been around in 1876, General George Armstrong Custer would have been the front-runner. He had been ordered not to attack. But hubris was too strong a part of Custer's character. He foolishly and fatally led his men into one of the largest slaughters in American History. His final words are variously reported as, "Hurrah boys, we've got them! We'll finish them up and then go back to our station," or "we've caught 'em napping." Both reflect the utterly fruitless scenario that has come down to us with the apropos moniker, "Custer's Last Stand," The Battle of Little Big Horn. General Custer's last actual known words were in a message, "Benteen. Come on. Big Village. Be quick, bring packs."

Another battle with Native Americans was the death of General Edward Braddock. Wrongly anticipating that he would live to fight another battle, he told his troops, "we shall know better how to deal with them the next time."

W. Somerset Maugham, English author of *The Razor's Edge* and other novels, said to a family member, "Death is a very dull, dreary affair. And I advise you to have nothing whatever to do with it."

One of the sacraments of the Catholic Church is Last Rights, where the dying are forgiven for the sins of life, anointed with oil (Extreme Unction), and prepared to meet their maker. Pietro Aretino, a Renaissance writer who was known as the "Scourge of Princes," said to his priest in respect to the oil, "keep the rats away now that I'm all greased up."

It's human nature to ask the sick how they're feeling. Usually, they lie. But Joel Chandler Harris, creator of Uncle Remus, Br'er Rabbit and Br'er Fox, the characters in his many books and the Disney film *Song of the South*, decided against it while also deciding not to split hairs. "I am feeling about the extent of a tenth of a gnat's eyebrow better."

Some visitors of the sick feel it necessary to lie to the dying and say they look like they are getting better, which occasionally elicits a statement like Henrik Ibsen's. The playwright author of *The Doll House* responded to just such a statement with, "On the contrary!"

Still other guests wish to fuss and fidget, which gained a "let me have my own fidgets!" from British journalist, Walter Bagehot, to someone who was trying to fluff his pillows.

Irish wit abounds again with the last words of author John Phillip Curran, whose doctor noticed that his coughing was worse. The doctor said it seemed that coughing was more difficult for him, to which he replied, "That's surprising, I've been practicing all night."

Recalling the epitaph of John Keats, Robbie Ross, one of the companions of Oscar Wilde, switched it up a bit with his final words, "Here lies one whose name was writ in hot water." (Oscar Wilde and many of the men he associated with were homosexuals during a time when being so was subject to criminal prosecution and incarceration.)

I'm not sure if fruit actually had anything to do with it, but Denis Diderot, another member of the pantheon of Enlightenment, was eating an apricot; his wife said he shouldn't. His last words: "What possible harm could it do to me?"

BIBLIOGRAPHY ❧

Comic Epitaphs: From the Very Best Old Graveyards. Mount Vernon, NY: Peter Pauper Press, 1957

Bergin, Edward. *The Definitive Guide to Underground Humor: Quaint Quotes about Death, Funny Funeral Home Stories, & Hilarious Headstone Epitaphs*. Waterbury, CT: Offbeat Publishing, 1996

Bisbort, Alan. *Famous Last Words: Apt Observations, Pleas, Curses, Benedictions, Sour Notes, Bon Mots, and Insights from People on the Brink of Departure*. San Francisco: Pomegranate Communication, 2001

Brown, Raymond Lamont. *A Book of Epitaphs*. New York, NY: Taplinger Pubishing Co., 1967

Gillies, Nicola, *The Last Word: Tombstone Wit and Wisdom*. Oxford: Past Times Press

Green, Jonathan. *Famous Last Words*. Prion, 2002

Greene, Janet. *Epitaphs to Remember: Remarkable Inscriptions from New England Gravestones*. Chambersburg, PA: Alan C. Hood & Co., Inc., 1962

Greene, Janet & Thomas C. Mann. *Sudden & Awful: American Epitaphs and the Finger of God*, Brattleboro, VT: The Stephen Greene Press, 1968

Haining, Peter. *The Graveyard Wit: The Humor of the Tombstone*, Newcastle Upon Tyne, England: Frank Graham, 1973

Hall, Alonzo C., *Grave Humor: A Collection of Humorous Epitaphs*. Charlotte, NC: McNally, 1961

Peter Haining, *The Graveyard Wit: The Humor of the Tombstone*, Frank Graham: Newcastle Upon Tyne, 1973

Everybody's Book of Epitaphs: Being for the Most Part What the Living Think of the Dead, W.H. Howe, ed. Kent, England: Pryor Publications, 1995

Lovric, Michelle. *Eccentric Epitaphs: Gaffe From Beyond the Grave*. New York: Barnes & Noble Books, 2000

Robinson, Ray. *Famous Last Words: Fond Farewells, Deathbed Diatribes, and Exclamations Upon Expiration*. New York: Workman Publishing Co., Inc, 2003

Ruffin, C. Bernard. *Last Words: A Dictionary of Deathbed Quotations*. Jefferson, NC: Macfarland & Co., 1995

Sax, Joel. http://www.alsirat.com/epitaphs/

Schafer, Louis S. *Best of Gravestone Humor*. New York, NY: Sterling Publishing Co., 1990

Shusan, E.R. *Grave Matters*. New York, NY: 1990

Slater, Scott & Alec Solomita. *Exits: Stories of Dying Moments and Parting Words*. New York, NY: E.P. Dutton, 1980

Spiegel, Fritz, ed. *A Small Book of Grave Humor*. New York: NY: Arco Publishing Co., Inc. 1973

Wallis, Charles L. *Stories on Stone: A Book of American Epitaphs*. New York, NY: Oxford University Press, 1954

Ward, Laura. *Famous Last Words: The Ultimate Collection of Finales and Farewells*. London: PRC Publishing Limited, 2004

INDEX ✺